Lucas–Preis

2015

Wie entsteht eine Schrift in der Forschung und in der Geschichte?

Die Hebräische Bibel und der Koran

von

Angelika Neuwirth

Übersetzungen von
Paul Silas Peterson

Herausgegeben von
Jürgen Kampmann

Mohr Siebeck

Angelika Neuwirth; geboren 1943; Studium der Arabistik, Islamwissenschaft und Klassischen Philologie in Berlin, Göttingen, Teheran, Jerusalem und München; 1972 Promotion; 1977 Habilitation; 1977–1983 Lehrtätigkeit an der University of Jordan; seit 1991 Inhaberin des Lehrstuhls für Arabistik an der Freien Universität Berlin; 1994–2000 Direktorin des Orient-Instituts in Beirut und Istanbul; Leiterin des Forschungsprojekts »Figurationen des Märtyrers« am Zentrum für Literatur- und Kulturforschung Berlin, des Forschungsprojekts »Von Logos zu Kalam« im Sonderforschungsbereich »Episteme in Bewegungen« an der Freien Universität Berlin, sowie des Forschungsprojekts »Corpus Coranicum – Dokumentierte Edition und literaturwissenschaftlich-historischer Kommentar« an der Berlin-Brandenburgischen Akademie der Wissenschaften.

ISBN 978-3-16-155242-7

Die Deutsche Nationalbibliothek verzeichnet diese Publikation in der Deutschen Nationalbibliographie; detaillierte bibliographische Daten sind im Internet über *http://dnb.dnb.de* abrufbar.

Das Buch wurde von Computersatz Staiger in Rottenburg/N. aus der Bembo gesetzt und von Gulde Druck in Tübingen gedruckt.

Inhalt

The Genesis of Scripture in Research
and in History
The Hebrew Bible and the Quran

by

Angelika Neuwirth

Wie entsteht eine Schrift in der Forschung
und in der Geschichte?
Die Hebräische Bibel und der Koran

von

Angelika Neuwirth

I

The Genesis of the Quran in Scholarship

The Leopold Lucas Prize, which I have the honor of receiving today, is a truly exceptional prize. I thank Dr. Frank Lucas, the grandson of the prize's founder, as well as the Protestant Faculty of Theology at the University of Tübingen, for the great honor that has been bestowed upon me today. To receive the Lucas Prize is, however, not only a matter of honor; at the same time it also puts the recipient to shame. This is because it comes from the hands of a family who were, as members of Judaism in Germany, subjected to an unparalleled and unspeakable injustice. Only the newly awakened memory of that which was nearly lost – the devotion to a distinctive, culturally-unifying mode of historical thought, which was cultivated in German Judaism, and which must be revived again today – can reach across the abyss of this catastrophe. This inclusive mode of thought, as we would call it today, was developed in the movement of the *Wissenschaft des Judentums*. The figure, whose memory is kept alive with this Prize, Dr. Leopold Lucas – the founder of the Gesellschaft zur Förderung der Wissenschaft des Judentums, who worked at the *Hochschule für die Wissenschaft des Juden-*

I
Die Entstehung des Korans in der Forschung

Der Dr. Leopold Lucas-Preis, den ich heute entgegennehmen darf, ist ein außergewöhnlicher Preis. Ich danke dem Enkel des Stifters, Herrn Frank Lucas, wie auch der Evangelisch-Theologischen Fakultät der Eberhard-Karls-Universität Tübingen für die große mir heute hier erwiesene Ehre. Den Lucas-Preis zu empfangen ist aber nicht nur ehrenvoll, sondern zugleich auch beschämend. Denn er kommt aus den Händen einer Familie, der als Angehörigen des Judentums in Deutschland beispielloses Unrecht angetan worden ist, für das es keine Worte gibt. Über den Abgrund dieser Katastrophe hinwegreichen kann nur eine von neuem aktivierte Erinnerung an das Fast-Verlorene, die Treue zu einem besonderen, kulturenvereinenden Geschichtsdenken, das im deutschen Judentum gepflegt worden ist und das es heute wieder zu beleben gilt. Entwickelt wurde dieses – wir würden heute sagen – inklusivistische Denken in der Wissenschaft des Judentums. Die Persönlichkeit, deren Gedächtnis mit dem Preis am Leben gehalten werden soll, Dr. Leopold Lucas, Begründer der Gesellschaft zur Förderung der Wissenschaft des Judentums, war bis zu seiner Deportation im Jahr

tums in Berlin until his deportation in 1942 — was one of the last great scholars of this important German-Jewish reform movement.

The discovery of the Quran

The *Wissenschaft des Judentums*[1] is not the subject of my lecture. However, one cannot speak about Quran research without beginning with this important German-Jewish intellectual movement. It was in the circle of this movement that the Quran was elevated to a subject of serious academic research for the first time. The Quran was not a purely academic discovery; it entered into the academic discourse in the context of a new philosophical reflection, a Jewish cultural criticism that was engaging Christianity.[2] The triangle of Judaism, Christianity and Islam was thus marked out from the beginning as the area of encounter and conflict of German Quran research. How then did the Quran become the Quran which we Western observers know today? Why does the Quran present us with such a different image than that which is presented to its readers within Islam? The following considerations on this matter can render plausibility to our attempt at reconstructing the genesis of the Quran presented in the second part of this lecture.

1942 als einer der letzten großen Gelehrten dieser bedeutenden deutsch-jüdischen Reformbewegung an der Hochschule für die Wissenschaft des Judentums in Berlin tätig.

Die Entdeckung des Koran

Die Wissenschaft des Judentums[1] ist nicht Thema meines Vortrags. Man kann aber nicht sinnvoll über Koranforschung sprechen, ohne mit dieser bedeutenden deutsch-jüdischen intellektuellen Bewegung zu beginnen. Denn in ihren Kreisen wurde der Koran erstmals zu einem Gegenstand ernsthafter wissenschaftlicher Forschung erhoben. Der Koran war keine rein akademische Entdeckung, sondern trat im Kontext einer weltanschaulichen Neubesinnung, einer jüdischen Kulturkritik, in Auseinandersetzung mit dem Christentum, in den wissenschaftlichen Diskurs ein.[2] Das Dreieck Judentum, Christentum und Islam ist damit als Spannungsfeld deutscher Koranforschung von vornherein abgesteckt. Wie ist der Koran also zu dem geworden, als der er sich uns westlichen Betrachtern heute darbietet? Warum bietet er uns ein so anderes Bild als seinen innerislamischen Lesern? Erst die nun folgenden Überlegungen dazu können den Versuch einer Rekonstruktion der Korangenese im zweiten Teil dieser Ausführungen plausibel machen.

The movement of the *Wissenschaft des Judentums* emerged at the beginning of the 19th century as a project involving a variety of academic disciplines. In this new branch of academic study, according to a contemporary of the founders, Immanuel Wolf, »the word Judaism is taken in its most comprehensive sense, taken as the epitome of all of the relationships, particularities and achievements of the Jews in relation to philosophy, history, law, literature, civil life and all human affairs – but not in a limited sense, in which this would only relate to the religion of the Jews.«[3] In this description one can clearly hear a universal objective which goes beyond the – already commendable and by no means uncontested – intention of an inner-Jewish reform. Full emancipation was only possible by entering the world of scholarship. In retrospect, the movement of *Wissenschaft des Judentums* was criticized for being antiquarian and distant from normal life.[4] It is true that for many of these scholars, philology, more than any other field of study, was the most viable path for ascertaining one's own identity. The challenge consisted in documenting one's own traditions in accordance with the then highly valued scholarly practice and in apologetically creating a space for it in the discourse of the time. One must recall that, at that time, the designation of a »Judeo-Christian Europe« which is so common today, and yet still pretentious, was not commonly used. One still spoke without hesitation of »the Christian Occident«. This use of words was no

Die Wissenschaft des Judentums war zu Anfang des 19. Jahrhunderts als pluridisziplinäres Projekt entworfen worden, bei dem – um einen Zeitgenossen der Gründer, Immanuel Wolf, zu Worte kommen zu lassen – »das Wort Judentum in seiner umfassendsten Bedeutung genommen wird, als Inbegriff der gesamten Verhältnisse, Eigenthümlichkeiten und Leistungen der Juden, in Beziehung auf Philosophie, Geschichte, Rechtswesen, Litteratur überhaupt, Bürgerleben und alle menschlichen Angelegenheiten – nicht aber in einem beschränkten Sinne, in welchem es nur die Religion der Juden bedeutet«.[3] Man hört hier deutlich eine – über die als solche bereits hoch verdienstvolle und keineswegs unumstrittene innerjüdische Reformabsicht hinausgehende – universale Zielsetzung heraus. Volle Emanzipation war nur über den Eintritt in die Welt der Wissenschaft denkbar. Man hat der Wissenschaft des Judentums aus der Retrospektive eine antiquarische, lebensferne Einstellung vorgeworfen.[4] In der Tat war für viele dieser Gelehrten mehr als alle anderen Wissenschaften Philologie der am ehesten gangbare Weg zur Selbstvergewisserung. Es galt, die eigenen Traditionen im Einklang mit der damals hochgeschätzten wissenschaftlichen Praxis zu dokumentieren, sie aber auch apologetisch in die Diskurse der Zeit einzubringen. Man muss sich vergegenwärtigen, dass es damals die heute so gängige – und dabei doch immer noch prätentiöse – Bezeichnung des »jüdisch-christlichen Europa« noch nicht gab, man sprach noch ganz

mere formality but also implied exclusion. Indeed, as indisputable as these universal values – which were mediated to this »Christian Occident« from the Bible – may have been, the actual heirs of the Bible were excluded from Western identity.[5] The *Wissenschaft des Judentums* was therefore concerned not least with disclosing the »other history« which was hidden and kept secret under the selectively established self-understanding of the non-Jewish majority society. The aim was establishing a cultural history of the world in which the Jewish legacy was to be made recognizable, in its importance and specificity, as a legacy to the West, to Europe. This inclusivist project was violently disrupted in Germany by the regime of terror under National Socialism. Before this, however, it was already confronted by severe attacks from pseudo-scientific anti-Jewish activities.[6] To this day the project is not finished. The new, analogical project of reflection on the Islamic heritage as a further legacy to Europe has still, for the most part, not been undertaken.

unbedenklich vom »christlichen Abendland«. Diese
Sprachregelung war keine bloße Formalie, sie be-
deutete auch Ausgrenzung. Denn so unbestritten die
von der Bibel an dieses christliche Abendland vermittelten universalen Werte auch sein mochten, die
eigentlichen Erben der Bibel waren von der abend-
ländischen Identität ausgeschlossen.[5] Es geht der
Wissenschaft des Judentums daher nicht zuletzt um
die Offenlegung der unter dem – selektiv begrün-
deten – Selbstverständnis der nicht-jüdischen Mehr-
heitsgesellschaft verborgenen und verschwiegenen
»anderen Geschichte«. Es geht um eine Welt-Kultur-
geschichte, in der das jüdische Erbe als Vermächtnis
an das Abendland, an Europa, in seiner Bedeutung
und Besonderheit erkennbar werden sollte. Dieses
inklusivistische Projekt wurde in Deutschland durch
das Terrorregime des Nationalsozialismus gewaltsam
abgebrochen, es war allerdings schon vorher, nicht
zuletzt durch pseudo-wissenschaftliche antijüdische
Umtriebe, harten Proben ausgesetzt gewesen.[6] Es ist
bis heute nicht abgeschlossen. Das neue, analoge Projekt der Reflexion über das islamische Erbe als eines
weiteren Vermächtnisses an Europa ist noch kaum
angegangen.

The embedding of the Quran
in the context of late antiquity

At an early period, the *Wissenschaft des Judentums* joined – harsh institutional resistance notwithstanding – the historical-critical method of research pursued in Christian theologies. That which was newly practiced and revolutionary in the 19th century – the reading of the Bible not as a religious but as a historical text – was also to be applied to their Hebrew text. In this regard, one may speak of two simultaneous re-readings of the Bible taking place in which scriptural texts were being drawn out of their centuries-old tradition of interpretation in the synagogue and in the church and transferred into the secular discipline of history. Yet why did Jewish scholars also include the Quran in the field of their historical approach (a step that would hardly have occurred to the Christian pioneers of the historical-critical method)? The reason for this has to do with their view of the world: for the Jews, the Quran was not situated in the »Remote East« but in the middle of their own culture of origin. For them (in contrast to the researchers acculturated in Christianity), Greco-Roman antiquity was not the »golden age«. For them, this was found in the Arab-Islamic past which was mostly unfamiliar to Europe – especially since the Ottoman conquests.

Die Einbettung des Koran
in einen spätantiken Kontext

Die Wissenschaft des Judentums schloss sich — allen institutionellen Widerständen zum Trotz — früh der in den christlichen Theologien verfolgten historisch-kritischen Forschungsrichtung an. Das, was im 19. Jahrhundert dort revolutionär neu praktiziert wurde, die Bibel nicht als religiösen, sondern als historischen Text zu lesen, sollte auch auf ihren hebräischen Text angewandt werden, so dass wir von zwei gleichzeitigen Neulektüren der Bibel sprechen können, durch welche Schrifttexte aus ihrer jahrhundertealten Deutungstradition in Synagoge und Kirche in die säkulare Disziplin der Geschichte überführt wurden. Doch warum bezogen jüdische Gelehrte auch den Koran in das Feld ihrer Historisierung ein — ein Schritt, der den christlichen Vorkämpfern für eine historisch-kritische Forschung kaum in den Sinn gekommen wäre? Die Gründe dafür sind weltanschaulich: Der Koran lag für die Juden nicht »im fernen Morgenland«, sondern in der Mitte ihrer eigenen Herkunftskultur. Für sie war nicht — wie für die christlich akkulturierten Forscher — die griechisch-römische Antike das Goldene Zeitalter, sondern die arabisch-islamische Vergangenheit, die für Europa (zumal seit den osmanischen Eroberungen) eher im Dunkel lag.

There were surely also external reasons. The practical exclusion of Jewish history and culture from the German *universitas litterarum* was an important impetus for thinking about an external self-positioning in the history of cultures. As is well known, into the 20th century there were no chairs for Jewish studies at German universities – despite the tireless efforts of Jewish historians.[7] For a long time, one could only enter the academic debate about Jewish cultural history »through the back door« of linguistic and Oriental studies. The memory of a particularly fruitful cultural synergy, indeed a »convivencia,«[8] between Jewish and Arab scholars in various periods and regions of Islamic cultural history was both substantial and decisive for the »Islamic past« option. Evidence of a highly sophisticated pre-modern symbiosis is found in an extensive library of Arabic-language works of Jewish authors[9] and also, beyond philosophy, in the fostering of the literary genres which were held to be characteristically Arabic and which were taken over into Hebrew, such as the Maqama, the Ghazal, or the mono-rhyme poem with its characteristic metres. Engaging with Arabic-language Islam was thus to study one's own cultural history. The architectural resonances of this new positioning of the golden age – which manifest themselves in the Andalusian patterns of synagogue buildings in the 19th century – are highly visible. Islamic culture had gained a unique partner in the circles of the *Wissenschaft des Judentums*.

Gewiss lieferten auch äußere Gründe, die faktische Exklusion jüdischer Geschichte und Kultur aus der deutschen *universitas litterarum*, einen wichtigen Anstoß, über eine externe Selbstpositionierung in der Geschichte der Kulturen nachzudenken. Bekanntlich gab es trotz unermüdlicher Vorstöße jüdischer Historiker[7] bis ins 20. Jahrhundert hinein keinen Lehrstuhl für Jüdische Studien an deutschen Universitäten. Man konnte jüdischer Kulturgeschichte lange Zeit nur »durch die Hintertür« sprachwissenschaftlicher und orientwissenschaftlicher Studien einen Einlass in die wissenschaftliche Debatte verschaffen. Substantiell war es aber die Erinnerung an eine besonders fruchtbare kulturelle Synergie, ja »convivencia«[8] zwischen jüdischen und arabischen Gelehrten in einzelnen Epochen und Regionen der islamischen Kulturgeschichte, die für die Option »Islamische Vergangenheit« ausschlaggebend war. Eine umfangreiche Bibliothek von arabischsprachigen Werken jüdischer Autoren,[9] über die Philosophie hinaus auch die ins Hebräische eingegangene Pflege von als typisch arabisch geltenden literarischen Gattungen wie die Maqame, das Ghasel oder das Monoreimgedicht mit seiner besonderen Metrik, legen von einer in der Vormoderne vollzogenen hoch anspruchsvollen Symbiose Zeugnis ab. Sich mit dem arabischsprachigen Islam zu befassen hieß also auch, eigene Kulturgeschichte zu betreiben. Die architektonischen Reflexe dieser Neupositionierung des Goldenen Zeital-

Abraham Geiger (1810–1874)

The positive impact of this Jewish engagement with Islamic studies, which was emerging at the beginning of the twentieth century, is undisputed. The work of Ignaz Goldziher (1850–1921), for example, set standards that are still respected today. The contribution of the *Wissenschaft des Judentums* in Quran research was soon forgotten, however. It was brought back to our consciousness only later, towards the end of the last century. It covers almost exactly 100 years, from 1833, the year of the publication of an inconspicuous dissertation titled *What did Mohammed draw from Judaism?* – written by a young Rabbi who would later become famous, Abraham Geiger – until 1933, the year of the National Socialist »Law for the Restoration of the Professional Civil Service« which expelled Jewish scholars from German universities. Geiger's work cannot be appreciated enough. It catapulted, as it were, the Quran to the rank of a challenging document in the research of the history of religions. Up

ters, die sich im Synagogenbau des 19. Jahrhunderts nach andalusischen Mustern manifestieren, sind unübersehbar. Die islamische Kultur hatte in den Kreisen der Wissenschaft des Judentums einen einzigartigen Partner gefunden.

Abraham Geiger (1810–1874)

Die positive Auswirkung dieses jüdischen Engagements auf die sich zu Anfang des 20. Jahrhunderts herausbildende Islamwissenschaft ist unbestritten, in der das Werk Ignaz Goldzihers (1850–1921) bis heute geltende Standards setzte. Die Einbringung der Wissenschaft des Judentums in die Koranforschung war dagegen bald vergessen und ist erst gegen Ende des letzten Jahrhunderts wieder ins Bewusstsein getreten. Sie erstreckte sich auf fast exakt 100 Jahre, nämlich von 1833, dem Jahr des Erscheinens einer unscheinbaren Dissertation mit dem Titel »Was hat Mohamed aus dem Judentume aufgenommen?« aus der Feder eines jungen Rabbiners, des später berühmten Abraham Geiger, bis 1933, dem Jahr des nationalsozialistischen »Gesetzes zur Wiederherstellung des Berufsbeamtentums«, das jüdische Gelehrte aus den deutschen Hochschulen ausschloss. Geigers Werk kann nicht hoch genug geschätzt werden, es katapultierte gewissermaßen den bis dahin (trotz Goethes

until this time, and despite Goethe's appreciation, the Quran was not at all recognized academically.

Geiger's historical-critical reading of the Quran can be called, without exaggeration, a founding achievement. For what initially appeared to be ambivalent in the other two traditions – the downgrading of the Holy Scriptures to the rank of texts that were relevant primarily with a view to historical research and the bracketing of their aura as transcendent revelations – was, in the case of the Quran, considered within its Western reception, an unmistakable upgrading. Given the generally negative assessment of Islam, and especially its founder, which extended even into the Enlightenment, the Quran, the founding document of this religion, was held to be a destructive and harmful text whose claim to transcendent inspiration had in any case been given no attention. Through Abraham Geiger's work it was now rehabilitated to the status of a value-neutral historic document like the other scriptures. That which was a break with tradition in Christian theology thus opened up new horizons in the research of the Quran! Moreover, through this historical reading, the Quran was given, for the first time, a specific context. It was taken from its homeland, which was deemed culturally narrow and marginal, and put into the great expanse of the debates of late antiquity. Due to many new discoveries, we know today that the Arabian Peninsula, and in particular the Hi-

Wertschätzung) akademisch gar nicht wahrgenommenen Koran auf den Rang eines religionshistorisch herausfordernden Dokuments.

Man kann bei Geigers historisch-kritischer Koranlektüre ohne Übertreibung von einer Gründungsleistung sprechen. Denn was in den beiden anderen Traditionen zunächst ambivalent erschien, die Herabstufung der Heiligen Schriften auf den Rang von primär historisch relevanten Texten, die Ausblendung ihrer Aura als transzendenter Botschaften, war im Fall des Koran – innerhalb seiner westlichen Rezeption betrachtet – unverkennbar eine Aufwertung: Der Koran, das Gründungsdokument des Islam, galt angesichts der generellen Negativbewertung dieser Religion, insbesondere ihres Stifters, die noch bis in die Aufklärung hineinreicht, als ein destruktiver, schädlicher Text, dessen Anspruch auf transzendente Inspiration ohnehin keine Beachtung erfahren hatte. Er wurde – durch Abraham Geigers Werk nun rehabilitiert – zu einer wertneutralen historischen Urkunde wie die anderen Schriften auch. Ein Traditionsbruch in der christlichen Theologie eröffnete also der Koranforschung neue Horizonte! Mehr noch, der Koran erhielt durch die historische Lektüre erstmals einen konkreten Kontext. Er wurde aus seiner kulturell als eng und marginal erachteten Heimat heraus in die Weite der spätantiken Debattenlandschaft geholt. Wir wissen heute aufgrund zahlreicher neuer Funde, dass die arabische Halbinsel und insbesondere der Hidjaz, keineswegs von der Kultur

jaz, was in no way cut off from the culture of the wider southern Mediterranean.[10] In the Quran especially, we see important debates from the broader Judeo-Christian cultural landscape.[11] Nevertheless, the Quran had been regarded, until then, as a piece of literature from the Arab periphery. It was first made recognizable as a voice in the concert of discussions of late antiquity with the scholars of the *Wissenschaft des Judentums*.

Consistent with his historical approach, Geiger could, of course, only see Muhammad as the »author« of the Quran. Mohammad's role as a proclaimer and negotiator of ideas did not interest him. The new context was not the Arabic milieu of the proclamation but the intellectual world of late antiquity. This perspective, which ignores the presence of listeners and their contribution to the development of the text – the ongoing negotiation and redefinition of *theologoumena* – necessarily brings a certain one-sidedness with it. At this time, an »author« (that was who Muhammad was to be) was held to be a creative genius (Geiger gives Mohammad a similar title »*Schwärmer*«), whose social conditions (in Muhammad's case, the acceptance of him by his audience) were not of particular interest. Consequently, everything that makes the Quran recognizable as a mirror of a gradual process of identity construction cannot come into view with Geiger. In itself, the Quran remains without development, its contemporary social embeddedness, the *Sitz im Leben* (social setting) of its individual mes-

des weiteren südlichen Mittelmeerraums abgeschnitten war;[10] vor allem erkennen wir im Koran wichtige Debatten der weiteren christlich-jüdischen Kulturlandschaft wieder.[11] Dennoch war der Koran bis dahin als ein Stück Literatur aus der arabischen Peripherie betrachtet worden – erst durch Gelehrte der Wissenschaft des Judentums wurde er als eine Stimme im Konzert der Diskussionen der Spätantike erkennbar gemacht.

Konsequent seinem historischen Ansatz kann Geiger natürlich Muhammad nur als »Autor« des Koran wahrnehmen, seine Rolle als Verkünder und Ideenverhandler interessierte ihn nicht. Der neue Kontext war nicht das arabische Milieu der Verkündigung, sondern die spätantike Geisteswelt. Diese Perspektive, die die Präsenz der Hörer und ihre Einbringung in die Entwicklung des Textes, die fortwährende Verhandlung und Neubestimmung von Theologumena, ignoriert, bringt notwendig eine gewisse Einseitigkeit mit sich: Ein »Autor« – das sollte Muhammad ja sein – galt zu jener Zeit als ein kreatives Genie (einen ähnlichen Titel, »Schwärmer«, spricht Geiger Muhammad auch zu), dessen soziale Bedingtheiten, in Muhammads Fall etwa seine Akzeptanz durch die Hörerschaft, kein besonderes Interesse beanspruchen konnten. Infolgedessen kann bei Geiger all das, was den Koran als Spiegel einer sukzessiven Identitätskonstruktion erkennbar macht, nicht in den Blick treten. Der Koran bleibt in sich selbst entwicklungslos, seine zeitgenössische soziale Einbettung, der »Sitz im Le-

sages, is not of interest. While the Quran is altogether the document of a reception, it is not – as was once polemically claimed – a reception of the Bible itself, but rather above all a reception of post-biblical exegesis. It is this affiliation, the exchange with the other post-biblical traditions reflected in the Quran, which gives it a new context, a place in the history of theology of late antiquity. Only due to the »inter-texts« (which Geiger and his school brought to light) – that is, the older traditions resonating in the Quran – it has become possible to recognize fully the Quranic »translation achievement«, the new interpretation of the then circulating forms of biblical exegesis. Although Geiger did not coin this expression, one can already find in Geiger a sense of the »epistemic space of late antiquity.« Today we are attempting to anchor the Quran in this anew, not as an authorial scripture but as a »transcript« of the genesis of a religion indebted to complex factors.

Geiger did not occupy himself again with the Quran after this work, which he wrote when he was 23 years old, in 1833, and which was, to some extent, »a stroke of genius.« Later he focused on the New Testament, the biblical scriptures and rabbinical works. It was left to his numerous successors, especially Josef Horovitz (1874–1931)[12] and his pupil Heinrich Speyer (1897–1935),[13] to develop his approach in the reference works which are still invaluable today. Al-

ben« seiner Einzelbotschaften, interessiert nicht. Der Koran ist ganz und gar das Dokument einer Rezeption, aber eben nicht, wie die Polemik vorher wollte, der Bibel selbst, sondern vor allem der postbiblischen Exegese. Es ist diese Affiliation, der im Koran reflektierte Austausch mit den anderen nachbiblischen Traditionen, die ihm einen neuen Kontext, einen Platz in der spätantiken Theologiegeschichte zuweist. Denn erst die von Geiger und seiner Schule ans Licht gebrachten »Intertexte«, die im Koran widerhallenden älteren Traditionen, machen es möglich, die koranische »Übersetzungsleistung«, die Neudeutung der im Umlauf befindlichen Bibelexegesen, in vollem Umfang zu erkennen. Ohne dass Geiger diesen Ausdruck geprägt hätte, kann man bei ihm bereits ein Gespür für den »Denkraum Spätantike« feststellen, in dem wir heute den Koran neu zu verankern versuchen – nun aber nicht als eine auktoriale Schrift, sondern als die »Mitschrift« einer komplexen Faktoren verdankten Religionsgenese.

Geiger selbst hat sich nach dem von ihm 1833 im Alter von 23 Jahren verfassten Werk, gewissermaßen einem »Geniestreich«, nicht weiter mit dem Koran befasst, sondern sich dem Neuen Testament, biblischen und rabbinischen Schriften zugewandt. Es sind seine zahlreichen Nachfolger, vor allem aber Josef Horovitz (1874–1931)[12] und dessen Schüler Heinrich Speyer (1897–1935)[13], die seinen Ansatz in noch heute unschätzbaren Referenzwerken weiterentwickelt ha-

most exactly 100 years of inter-textual Quran research from Jewish scholars – more was not available
due to the political circumstances – laid the incontro-
vertible foundation for that which we today pursue as
an urgent *desideratum*: the development of an understanding of the Quran that brings the text back into
the discursive space of the other monotheistic religions in late antiquity.

In this intellectual context, the Hebrew Bible is
the reference text *par excellence*. It is not only this in
terms of its grand narratives of creation and liberation, but in particular, in the hermeneutic sense, by
virtue of its immanent »typological« character. It is
unmistakable, as Felix Körner emphasizes,

[...] that the Bible as such – unlike other presentations of
sequences of events (chronicles, annals), such as those written in Greek or in other concurrent cultures – claims to see
a sense of direction in what is happening. The biblically
testified history of Israel was extremely volatile. Nevertheless, Israel could understand the events as coherently in-
terconnected. »Historical consciousness« itself was formed
in other cultures of reflection only after Israel's own pattern of self-understanding. [...] Each event has a character
of anticipation, is a preliminary-event of the end which is
hoped for. This is true for different events with varying
intensity.[14]

This immanent tension in the Hebrew Bible was first
made effective for its use in arguments and textual
strategies of interpretation in the »typological read-

ben. Fast genau 100 Jahre intertextuelle Koranforschung jüdischer Gelehrter – mehr standen aufgrund der politischen Umstände nicht zur Verfügung – haben die unumstößliche Basis gelegt für das, was wir heute wieder als dringendes Desiderat verfolgen: die Erarbeitung eines Koranverständnisses, das den Text in einen den monotheistischen Religionen gemeinsamen spätantiken Denkraum zurückholt.

In diesem Denkraum ist die hebräische Bibel der Referenztext schlechthin. Sie ist es nicht etwa nur hinsichtlich ihrer großen Erzählungen von Schöpfung und Befreiung, sie ist es insbesondere hermeneutisch, kraft ihres immanent »typologischen« Charakters. Es ist unverkennbar – wie Felix Körner hervorhebt –

[...] dass die Bibel als solche, anders als die auf Griechisch oder in anderen gleichzeitigen Kulturkreisen verfassten Darstellungen von Ereignisreihen (Chroniken, Annalen) den Anspruch erhebt, eine Sinnrichtung im Geschehen zu sehen: Das biblisch bezeugte Ergehen Israels war außerordentlich wechselhaft. Dennoch konnte Israel die Ereignisse als Zusammenhang verstehen. ›Geschichtliches Bewusstsein‹ überhaupt bildete sich in anderen Reflexionskulturen erst aus dieser Verständnishaltung Israels. [...] Jedes Ereignis hat einen Vorgriffscharakter, ist Vorweg-Ereignung des erhofften Endes. Das gilt aber für unterschiedliche Ereignisse in unterschiedlicher Intensität.[14]

Diese der hebräischen Bibel immanente Spannung wurde argumentativ und textstrategisch aber erst wirksam gemacht in den »typologischen Lektü-

ings« of biblical stories in late antiquity, as »Scriptures« emerged as the supreme authority over all
things. Guy Stroumsa has identified this new orientation as a »religious mutation of late antiquity.«[15] »Typological thinking« – understood as the reading of
traditions with a view to their immanent »anticipa-
tory character« – is also clearly reflected in the Quran.
There it takes, as will be shown, ever more refined
and also politically significant forms in the course
of its development. However, since the Quran, unlike the Hebrew Bible, does not provide a continuous narrative, and since the traces of its development
were almost entirely erased through the mechanical
arrangement of the suras (based on the length of the
texts) in the official codex (the *muṣḥaf*), the typological tension will only become fully recognizable after a restoration of a coherence of the text through
its chronological reconstruction. Geiger himself did
not have this aspect in view. With his historical readings, however, which (once they are brought into a
chronological order) depict a gradual appropriation
of older traditions, he did open up a path for the discovery of this particular hermeneutical dimension of
the Quran.

ren« biblischer Geschichten in der Spätantike, als »die Schrift« als die alles überragende Autorität entdeckt worden war,[15] eine Neuorientierung, die Guy Stroumsa als eine »religiöse Mutation der Spätantike« identifiziert hat. Das »typologische Denken« – verstanden als das Lesen von Traditionen auf den ihnen immanenten »Vorgriffscharakter« hin – reflektiert sich deutlich auch im Koran, es nimmt dort, wie gezeigt werden soll, im Laufe der Entwicklung immer raffiniertere, auch politisch signifikante Formen an. Da der Koran jedoch anders als die hebräische Bibel keine kontinuierliche Narrative bietet und da auch die Spuren seiner Entwicklung durch die mechanische, an der Textlänge orientierte Anordnung der Suren im offiziellen Kodex, dem *muṣḥaf*, fast gänzlich verwischt sind, wird die typologische Spannung erst nach Wiederherstellung einer Kohärenz des Textes durch seine chronologische Rekonstruktion voll erkennbar. Geiger selbst hat diesen Aspekt nicht im Blick gehabt, hat aber mit seiner historischen Lektüre, die – einmal in eine chronologische Reihenfolge gebracht – eine sukzessive Aneignung älterer Traditionen abbildet, den Weg zur Aufdeckung dieser besonderen hermeneutischen Dimension des Koran freigemacht.

An opposite break with tradition in Islam

Another path was taken in the intra-Islamic context. The lack of coherence in the canonical corpus,
and thus the typological tension, was compensated
for by a grand extra-Quranic narrative, the *Life of the
Prophet*, the *sīra*, which was presented literarily as a
part of a history of the world.[16] This placement of
the Quranic event in history, which came about 150
years after the Prophet's death, represents a decisive
turning point in the perception of the Quran. For
with this development the Quran is now read tele-
ologically towards the triumphant breakthrough of
Islam – a perspective that, of course, implies a re-
classification of the actors who were involved in the
genesis. Here the dichotomy is constructed which
thereafter organizes the followers and the opponents
of the prophet into two opposing worlds. The de-
feated – especially the pre-Islamic pagans – represent
the »world of ignorance« or »barbarism,« *Djāhiliyya*,
whose voices no longer matter in the new period.
The »people of the book,« many of whom had proven
to be opponents towards the end of the mission of the
Prophet, also receive a generally negative assessment.
That which had been often triumphantly declared in
the text – that the proclamation brought light into
the darkness (a perception that echoes that of earlier
prophets) – became, with the *sīra*, the backbone of a
new ideology. The *sīra* is a para-text to the Quran
whose neglect is unimaginable in the intra-Islamic

Ein gegenläufiger Traditionsbruch im Islam

Innerislamisch war ein anderer Weg beschritten worden. Die dem kanonischen Corpus fehlende Kohärenz und damit typologische Spannung war hier durch eine große extra-koranische Erzählung, die Prophetenvita, die *Sīra*, literarisch angelegt als Teil einer Weltgeschichte, kompensiert worden.[16] Diese etwa 150 Jahre nach dem Tode des Propheten vorgenommene Einordnung des koranischen Events in die Geschichte stellt eine entscheidende Wende in der Wahrnehmung des Koran dar. Denn nun wird der Koran teleologisch auf den triumphalen Durchbruch des Islam hin gelesen, eine Perspektive, die naturgemäß eine Neueinstufung der an der Genese beteiligten Akteure impliziert. Es wird dazu jene Dichotomie konstruiert, die hinfort Anhänger und Gegner des Propheten zwei konträren Welten zuordnet. Die Besiegten — vor allem die vorislamischen Paganen — repräsentieren die »Welt der Unwissenheit« oder »Barbarei« (*Djāhiliyya*), deren Stimmen in der neuen Zeit nicht mehr zählen. Auch die »Leute der Schrift«, von denen sich viele gegen Ende der Mission des Propheten als Gegner erwiesen hatten, erfahren generell eine Negativ-Wertung. Was im Text selbst öfter triumphal festgestellt worden war, dass mit der Verkündigung Licht in ein Dunkel getragen worden war — eine Wahrnehmung, die diejenige früherer Propheten nachhallen lässt — wurde mit der *Sīra* zum Rückgrat einer neuen Ideologie. Die *Sīra* ist ein

context. By providing a rough timeline of the proc-
lamations, it resituates the Quranic event in a historical context. This is, however, derived less from a reconstruction of the individual events than from in-
ferences to the victory of Islam, which had by then
become a historical fact. The *sīra* has been called the
»gospel of the Quran,« insofar as it puts the Quranic
statements into a narrative.

Nevertheless, one cannot speak here of a closure
of the process of textual interpretation. A relativi-
zation of the *sīra*-interpretation was brought about
through the reflections of exegetes who attributed a
plurality of meanings to every single verse, regard-
less of *sīra*-guidelines, while also frequently falling
back upon Jewish and Christian traditions. Even a
genre of commentary was formed which was later
polemically referred to as *Isrā'īliyyāt*.[17] It focused on
the depositories of knowledge of the Jews and Christians which were to contribute to the elucidation of
the – often narrated in a truncated form – biblical
stories in the Quran. In many cases, these explana-
tions brought precisely those post-biblical interpretations of the Hebrew Bible back into the text which
were to have been relativized through the original
proclamation. The dimension of a critique of religion
in the proclamation was largely blurred by this genre
of commentary. Being read through the lens of the

innerislamisch nicht wegzudenkender Paratext zum Koran. Indem sie eine grobe Chronologie der Verkündigungen vornimmt, gibt sie dem koranischen Event eine historische Einbettung zurück, die sich allerdings weniger aus der Rekonstruktion der Einzelereignisse als aus Rückschlüssen aus dem inzwischen zum historischen Faktum gewordenen Sieg des Islam ableitet. Von der *Sīra* ist als dem »Evangelium des Koran« gesprochen worden, insofern sie die koranischen Aussagen in eine Narrative kleidet.

Dennoch kann von einer Schließung des Textverständnisses keine Rede sein. Eine Relativierung erfuhr die *Sīra*-Deutung nämlich durch die Reflektionen der Exegeten, die ohne Rücksicht auf *Sīra*-Vorgaben jedem einzelnen Vers eine Mehrzahl von Bedeutungen zuwiesen und dabei auch häufig auf jüdische und christliche Traditionen zurückgriffen. Es bildete sich sogar eine eigene Kommentargattung heraus — später polemisch als *Isrāʾīliyyāt*[17] bezeichnet —, die sich auf die Wissensbestände der Juden und Christen konzentrierte, die zur Erhellung der im Koran narrativ oft knapp erzählten biblischen Geschichten beitragen sollten. Diese Erklärungen trugen nun in vielen Fällen diejenigen nachbiblischen Deutungen der Hebräischen Bibel wieder in den Text hinein, die durch die Verkündigung gerade hatten relativiert werden sollen. Die religionskritische Dimension der Verkündigung wurde durch diese Kommentargattung weitgehend wieder ausgelöscht. Der Koran

Isrā'īliyyāt, the Quran turned from being a text of reform to a text of edification.

Although the *Isrā'īliyyāt*-exegesis often agrees with
Geiger's findings, they are both indebted to entirely
different approaches. The Islamic exegetes were
certain of their sovereign command over the registers of knowledge of late antiquity. Those Jewish
and Christian traditions which they brought to the
Quran were a part of their epistemic world and could
therefore legitimately be drawn upon to illuminate
the Quran. They were not concerned with the origins of these traditions; indeed, these stemmed, like
the knowledge attested in the Quran itself, from that
comprehensive and homiletically processed oral tradition, which Sidney Griffith persuasively calls the
»interpreted Bible«.[18]

By contrast, Geiger sees in the Quran and in the
Messenger a belated recipient of his own tradition.
Geiger measures – entirely in the spirit of the 19th
century – the »correctness« of the Quranic reflections
of earlier traditions by the wordings of the »origi-
nals,« that is, the Jewish traditions, and therefore
often comes to negative critical assessments of the
Quran. The older versions he identified remain the
privileged text. In his linking together of post-biblical and Quranic traditions, Geiger did not pursue a
theological interest in his comparison of the versions.
Despite its limitation to the collection and philological explanation of earlier traditions echoing in the

wurde – durch die Linse der *Isrāʾīliyyāt* gelesen – aus einem reformatorischen zu einem erbaulichen Text.

Obwohl sich die *Isrāʾīliyyāt*-Exegesen nicht selten mit Geigerschen Funden treffen, verdanken sich beide doch einem gänzlich verschiedenen Denken. Die islamischen Exegeten waren sich gewiss, über das spätantike Wissen souverän verfügen zu dürfen – die von ihnen an den Koran herangeführten jüdischen und christlichen Traditionen sind Teil ihrer epistemischen Welt und daher legitimerweise zur Erhellung des Koran heranziehbar. Die Herkunft der Überlieferungen interessiert sie nicht – sie entstammen ja wie das im Koran selbst verhandelte Wissen der umfassenden mündlichen, homiletisch bereits aufbereiteten Tradition, von der Sidney Griffith überzeugend als »interpreted Bible«[18] gesprochen hat.

Dagegen sieht Geiger im Koran und im Verkünder einen spät gekommenen Rezipienten seiner eigenen Tradition. Geiger misst – ganz im Geist des 19. Jahrhunderts – die »Richtigkeit« der koranischen Reflexe früherer Traditionen an den Wortlauten der »Originale«, das heißt an den jüdischen Traditionen, und kommt daher oft zu kritischen Negativeinschätzungen des Koran. Die von ihm identifizierten älteren Fassungen bleiben der privilegierte Text. Ein theologisches Interesse an einem Vergleich der Versionen hegt Geiger bei seiner Zusammenführung postbiblischer und koranischer Tradition nicht. Trotz seiner Begrenztheit auf die Sammlung und philolo-

Quran, Geiger's work, however, addressed the center of interest of his time in Western research, when questions concerning the history of religions were controversially discussed, even in the public sphere.[19]

Understandably, a theological interest in neighboring traditions is also lacking on the Islamic side. Although in the classical period scholars had written works about other religions from the twelfth century onward,[20] and later even provided approaches towards a textual comparison between the Quran and the Hebrew Bible,[21] these were not programmatically oriented toward the entire text, and were not sufficiently sustained to initiate a systematic-theological comparison. This comparison was not held to be a *desideratum* for the exegetes because here as well the privileged version of the text was undisputed. The Quran had come as the final and decisive scripture to humanity. Furthermore, with its Arabic garb it gave a compelling and final shape to the monotheistic traditions which were until then circulating in different languages. Why search for the original forms of the truths of the faiths of others when the Quran had already been substituted in place of them? That this did happen at a later time, for example, with al-Biqā'ī (d. 1480), is the result of a reform movement.[22] This movement brought older depositories of knowledge back into consciousness at a time of political and social crisis, without, however, initiating a broad renewal of Quranic exegesis. What Geiger's Western

gische Erklärung der im Koran nachhallenden früheren Traditionen stieß Geigers Werk in der westlichen Forschung aber ins Zentrum des Interesses seiner Zeit, in der religionsgeschichtliche Fragen sogar in der Öffentlichkeit kontrovers ausgetragen wurden.[19]

Ein theologisches Interesse an den Nachbartraditionen fehlt begreiflicherweise auch auf islamischer Seite. Wenngleich es bereits in klassischer Zeit seit dem 12. Jahrhundert gelehrte Werke über andere Religionen[20] und später sogar Ansätze zu einem Textvergleich zwischen Koran und hebräischer Bibel[21] gegeben hat, waren diese doch nicht programmatisch auf den gesamten Text ausgerichtet, vor allem aber nicht nachhaltig genug, um einen systematischen theologischen Abgleich anzustoßen. Dieser Abgleich war für die Exegeten auch kein Desiderat, denn auch hier stand die privilegierte Textform fest. Der Koran war als die letzte, entscheidende Schrift an die Menschheit gekommen; er hatte zudem durch seine arabische Einkleidung den bis dahin in verschiedenen Sprachen kursierenden monotheistischen Traditionen eine überzeugende und letztgültige Form gegeben. Warum also nach den Originalformen der im Koran ja bereits substituierten Glaubenswahrheiten der anderen forschen? Dass dies – etwa durch al-Biqāʿī (gest. 1480) in späterer Zeit dennoch geschah, verdankt sich einer Aufbruchbewegung,[22] die in einer Zeit der politisch-sozialen Krise alte Wissensbestände wieder ins Bewusstsein hob, ohne allerdings eine breite Erneuerung der Koranexegese anzusto-

readers in the nineteenth century saw as a widening of the horizon would have been seen in the Islamic world (if it could ever have arrived there), as at best a reworking of the *Isrā'īliyyāt*. The contextualization of the Quran among other biblical traditions lay already behind them. It had been a welcome exegetical support for the mainstream theologians, and for the so-called »Hebraists« among the exegetes it had also been a challenge. Hermeneutically, however, it did not provide an impetus for a historical understanding of the Quran. In orthodox groups it had long fallen into disrepute and among the reformists in the nineteenth century it was severely frowned upon.

While the break with tradition, which came with the historical understanding of the Scriptures, was thus an important step towards modern theologies in Christianity and Judaism, Geiger's corresponding reading of the Quran was entirely irrelevant to Islam. Not only did any mediation of the new approach fail to materialize with respect to the Quran, restrictive steps were also taken to limit significantly the range of its possible interpretations. This indicates, in my opinion, an almost tragic mistake on the part of the Arabic Quran scholars. To be sure, a break with tradition also occurred in the Islamic world during the 19th century. But instead of establishing a new (historical) universe of interpretation, this led, by means of a comprehensive act of forgetting, to a substantial

ßen. Was für Geigers westliche Leser im 19. Jahrhundert eine Weitung des Horizonts war, wäre in der islamischen Welt, wäre es dort angekommen, also allenfalls als eine Neuaufbereitung von *Isrā'īliyyāt* angesehen worden. Man hatte die Kontextualisierung des Koran mit den biblischen Traditionen schon hinter sich, sie war für die Mainstream-Theologen eine willkommene exegetische Hilfestellung gewesen, für die sogenannten »Hebraisten« unter den Exegeten auch eine Herausforderung, hatte aber hermeneutisch keinen Anstoß zu einer historischen Wahrnehmung des Koran gegeben. Sie war in orthodoxen Kreisen auch längst in Misskredit geraten und unter den Reformdenkern des 19. Jahrhunderts gänzlich verpönt.

Während der mit dem historischen Verständnis der heiligen Schriften in Kauf genommene Traditionsbruch für das Christentum und Judentum also einen wichtigen Schritt hin zu einer modernen Theologie darstellte, war die entsprechende Koranlektüre Geigers für den Islam gänzlich irrelevant. Nicht nur blieb die Vermittlung des neuen Ansatzes aus, es wurden vor Ort auch restriktive Weichen gestellt, die das Spektrum der möglichen Koranlektüren erheblich einschränken sollten. Damit ist ein meines Erachtens geradezu tragischer Fehlgriff der arabischen Korangelehrten angesprochen. Denn es hatte auch in der islamischen Welt im 19. Jahrhundert durchaus ein Bruch mit der Tradition stattgefunden. Dieser hatte aber – statt ein neues (historisches) Deutungsuniver-

curtailing of the Quran in its range of impact. For with the inner-Islamic cultural break – which was brought about with the Quran commentaries since 1900 by the reformers Muḥammad 'Abduh (1849–1905)[23] and Rashīd Riḍā (1865–1935)[24] – a step was taken for the Quran which had already been taken in Protestant theology, namely the rejection of the tradition of interpretation as obscuring the text, indeed as obsolete.[25] With this dislocating of the text, its »dis-embedding«, if you will, out of its exegetical tradition came an absolutization of the Quran, unprecedented in the history of Islam, as a canon of norms. The intra-Islamic interpretation of the Quran had prided itself as an infinite sea, an »ocean of (mutually relativizing) interpretations,« *baḥr min al-ma'ānī*.[26] This had provided Quran scholarship with that flexibility that Thomas Bauer, in his monograph *The Culture of Ambiguity*, aptly called the »tolerance of ambiguity.« In place of the diverse interpretations, including allegorical and typological interpretations, with the reform came the *one* literal sense. Thereby the Quran assumed those rigid traits which opened it up for fundamentalist interpretations. It became fixed as an unquestioned source of timelessly applicable norms and can therefore appear to many Muslims today as a kind of law book.[27]

sum zu eröffnen – dazu geführt, den Koran durch einen umfassenden Akt des Vergessens in seiner Wirkungsweite substantiell zu beschneiden. Denn mit dem innerislamischen Kulturbruch, durchgesetzt mit dem seit 1900 erscheinenden Korankommentar der Reformer Muḥammad ʿAbduh (1849–1905)[23] und Rashīd Riḍā (1865–1935)[24], wurde vor allem ein in der protestantischen Theologie vollzogener Schritt – die Abstoßung der auslegenden Tradition insgesamt als den Text verunklärend, ja obsolet – für den Koran nachvollzogen.[25] Mit dieser »Entbettung« des Textes aus seiner exegetischen Tradition einher ging eine in der Islamgeschichte beispiellose Verabsolutierung des Koran als Normenkanon. Die innerislamische Koranauslegung hatte sich stolz als ein »unendliches Meer« verstanden, als ein »Ozean von (einander relativierenden) Deutungen«, als *baḥr min al-maʿānī*.[26] Sie hatten der Korangelehrsamkeit jene Flexibilität vermittelt, die Thomas Bauer in seiner Monographie »Die Kultur der Ambiguität« treffend als »Ambiguitätstoleranz« bezeichnet hat. An die Stelle der vielfältigen Deutungen, darunter allegorischen und typologischen, trat damit der *eine* Literalsinn, durch den der Koran nun jene starren Züge annahm, die ihn für fundamentalistische Auslegungen öffnen sollte. Er wurde zu einer unhinterfragten Quelle zeitlos geltender Normen verfestigt und kann daher heute vielen Muslimen als eine Art Gesetzbuch erscheinen.[27]

The Quran after the disruption
of historical research

Two breaks with tradition with very different, indeed contrary consequences for the perception of the
Holy Scriptures! Despite personal contacts of individual researchers to Arab and Indian colleagues,[28]
despite occasional cooperation especially in the work
on editions,[29] Quran research was to take place in
East and West in the 19th and early 20th century in
two largely unconnected worlds. It must be called
an »accident of history« that cooperation across the
borderlines first began only after the forced exit of
the Jewish scholars from the stage of German scholarship. This stage was now, after the expulsion of the
Jewish scholars, newly set. After the loss of the textual research (which they suspected to be mere tink-
ering anyway), the remaining Arabists at the German universities – who lacked the linguistic and cul-
tural-historical prerequisites for historical Quran
research and who were neither conversant in a plurality of Semitic languages nor the religious traditions of late antiquity – quickly took solace in a »life
of Muhammad research.«[30] Here the source was no
longer primarily the Quran but the Islamic narrative
of early Islam. Not the Quran's context of late an-

Der Koran nach dem Abbruch
der historischen Forschung

Es begegnen also zwei Traditionsbrüche mit ganz verschiedenen, ja gegenläufigen Konsequenzen für die Wahrnehmung der heiligen Schrift! Trotz persönlicher Kontakte einzelner Forscher zu arabischen und indischen[28] Kollegen, trotz gelegentlicher Zusammenarbeit vor allem im Editionswesen[29] vollzog sich Koranforschung in Ost und West im 19. und frühen 20. Jahrhundert noch in zwei weitgehend unvernetzten Welten. Es ist als ein »Unfall der Geschichte« zu bezeichnen, dass es zu einer Zusammenarbeit erst nach dem Abtritt der jüdischen Wissenschaftler von der Bühne der deutschen Wissenschaft kam. Diese Bühne wurde jetzt, nach der Vertreibung der jüdischen Gelehrten, neu besetzt: Die an den Universitäten verbliebenen Arabisten, denen die sprachlichen und kulturgeschichtlichen Voraussetzungen für die historische Koranforschung fehlten, denen weder eine Mehrzahl von semitischen Sprachen noch die religiösen Traditionen der Spätantike zur Verfügung standen, trösteten sich rasch über den Verlust der ihnen ohnehin als Tüftelei verdächtigen Textarbeit. Sie wandten sich nun einer »Leben Muhammad-Forschung«[30] zu, deren Quelle nicht mehr

tiquity but the canonized Islamic picture of history was to matter. The pendulum swung from a focus on the biblical tradition to a focus on the autochthonous Arab-Islamic tradition. In comparison to its predecessor, this research has been criticized as amnesia of method. It is also true, however, that it was immediately understood and accepted by traditional Muslim scholars in the Arab world who had likewise drawn upon the Islamic narrative. For some decades, even traditional Arab universities were open to the teaching and research of European Islam researchers – a situation which is no longer imaginable today.

This academic symbiosis was shaken in its foundations by a sudden change of climate in East-West relations. This was not primarily because of political differences but because of a »text war,« specifically the publication of two English-language monographs with explosive content that triggered the shock. In 1977 three critical historians, John Wansbrough,[31] Patricia Crone[32] and Michael Cook, radically challenged the Quran research that was oriented towards the history of Islam. Not only did they question the traditional dating of the Quran genesis in the early seventh century, they also declared the historicity of the entire narrative of the emergence of the Quran (as a proclamation presented by Muhammad to a com-

primär der Koran, sondern die islamische Narrative
vom Frühislam war. Nicht mehr der spätantike Kontext des Koran, sondern das islamisch kanonisierte
Bild der Geschichte sollte ausschlaggebend sein. Das
Pendel schlug von der Fokussierung der biblischen
Tradition wieder um zu einer Fokussierung der au-
tochthon-arabisch-islamischen. Man hat dieser Forschung im Vergleich zu ihrem Vorgänger Methoden-
vergessenheit vorgeworfen, Faktum ist aber auch,
dass sie von traditionellen muslimischen Gelehrten
in der arabischen Welt verstanden und akzeptiert
wurde, die sich ja ebenfalls auf die islamische Narrative beriefen. Für einige Jahrzehnte standen daher
europäischen Islamforschern sogar traditionell-ara-
bische Universitäten zu Lehre und Forschung offen
– eine heute nicht mehr vorstellbare Situation.

Diese akademische Symbiose wurde durch einen
plötzlichen Klimasturz in den ost-westlichen Beziehungen in ihren Grundlagen erschüttert. Es waren
dabei gar nicht primär politische Differenzen, sondern ein »Textkrieg«, konkret das Erscheinen von
zwei englischsprachigen Monographien mit explosi-
vem Inhalt, die den Schock auslösten: 1977 rechneten
drei kritische Historiker, John Wansbrough[31], Patricia Crone[32] und Michael Cook radikal mit der an
Islam-Geschichte orientierten Koranforschung ab,
indem sie nicht nur die traditionelle Datierung der
Korangenese ins frühe 7. Jahrhundert infrage stellten,
sondern die Historizität der gesamten Entstehungs-
narrative des Koran als einer von Muhammad einer

munity of listeners) to be a myth. In place of the
Islamic narratives (indeed even in place of the basic data regarding the proclamation of the Prophet
in Mecca and then in Medina) came a *tabula rasa*.
Their epistemic pessimism with respect to the historical reports (which were written about a century
after the events) led the group of »skeptical scholars«
to a minimalist view of the picture of the Quran's
genesis, ruling out the entire narrative of the Islamic
tradition. Since there did not seem to exist certain
knowledge about the time before its codification, the
Quran makes its appearance, according to them, as
an already completed text. While it could be attributed to various social constellations, it could best be
explained as an anonymous compilation, prepared
for a Jewish-Christian community in Mesopotamia
or Syria. The Quran – a kind of post-biblical apo-
crypha? This view, which has dominated the research
of early Islam for about 20 years, not only unsettled
a Western tradition of research but also drove a deep
wedge between Quran research in the East and in the
West.

But was a true breakthrough achieved with this
skepticism? Had not simply *one* foreknowledge, *one*
teleology, been replaced by another? Wasn't the intra-Islamic notion of the Quran as a divinely-willed
beginning of all relevant history replaced by the idea
of a scriptural text deliberately composed by an author or team of authors for the construction of a new

Hörergemeinde vorgetragenen Verkündigung zum Mythos erklärten. An die Stelle der islamischen Narrative, ja sogar der Basisdaten – Verkündigung durch den Propheten in Mekka, dann in Medina – tritt damit eine *tabula rasa*. Ihr epistemischer Pessimismus angesichts der erst etwa ein Jahrhundert nach den Ereignissen verschriftlichten historischen Berichte führte die skeptizistischen Forscher zu einer minimalistischen Sicht auf das Szenario der Korangenese, die nun die gesamte in der islamischen Tradition vertretene Interpretation ausblendete. Da kein sicheres Wissen über die Zeit vor der Kodifizierung vorzuliegen schien, tritt der Koran für sie erst als fertiger Text in Erscheinung, der sich verschiedenen sozialen Konstellationen verdanken konnte, der aber am ehesten als eine anonyme Kompilation, hergestellt für eine judenchristliche Gemeinde in Mesopotamien oder Syrien, erklärbar erschien. Der Koran – eine Art postbiblischer Apokryphe? Diese die Frühislamforschung etwa 20 Jahre lang dominierende Sicht erschütterte nicht nur eine westliche Forschungstradition, sie trieb auch einen tief einschneidenden Keil zwischen die Koranforschung in Ost und West.

War mit dem Skeptizismus aber ein wirklicher Durchbruch erreicht? War nicht einfach *ein* Vorauswissen, *eine* Teleologie, durch eine andere ersetzt worden: die innerislamische Vorstellung vom Koran als göttlich gewollter Anfang relevanter Geschichte durch die Vorstellung einer mit Vorbedacht von einem Autor oder Autorenkollektiv kompilier-

biblically-shaped identity? In both perspectives the Quran has no development; it is rather a static *fait accompli*, a »mere book« – a truncated presentation of the concept of »Holy Scripture,« in a manner that would be unheard of in biblical research. The epistemic price for this experiment with the Quran's genesis is thus significant, but the political price was high, too; the bridges between the two cultures of interpretation have since been long broken.

A turn in Oriental Studies:
A new approach after the 11th
of September 2001

Must the particular sensitivities of the Muslim scholars matter in Western academic research? There has long been an attempt at bracketing the political dimension of the Middle Eastern history of ideas from the debate. That is no longer possible today. After the shock of the attacks of the 11th of September our academic landscape also changed. A new public reflection about Islam and the Quran set in that had allegedly remained »unknown.« This put important new research initiatives into motion. One of the first major projects was initiated at the Berlin-Brandenburg Academy of Sciences in 2007, the *Corpus Coranicum*: *Textual Documentation and Historical-Literary Commen-*

ten Schrift zur Konstruktion einer neuen biblisch geprägten Identität? In beiden Perspektiven kennt der Koran keine Entwicklung, ist vielmehr ein statisches *fait accompli*, ein »Nur-Buch« – eine verstümmelte Vorstellung des Begriffs »Heilige Schrift«, wie sie in der Bibelforschung unerhört wäre. Der epistemische Preis für dieses Experiment mit der Korangenese ist also erheblich, doch auch der politische Preis war hoch; die Brücken zwischen den beiden Interpretationskulturen sind seither für lange Zeit abgebrochen.

Eine Wende der Orientwissenschaften: Ein neuer Zugang nach dem 11. September 2001

Muss aber die besondere Befindlichkeit der muslimischen Gelehrten die westliche akademische Forschung tangieren? Man hat lange versucht, die politische Dimension der nahöstlichen Ideengeschichte aus der Debatte auszublenden. Das ist heute nicht mehr möglich. Nach dem Schock der Attentate des 11. September 2001 hat sich auch unsere akademische Landkarte verschoben. Ein neues öffentliches Nachdenken über den offenbar »unbekannt« gebliebenen Islam und Koran setzte ein, das wichtige neue Forschungsinitiativen in Gang setzte. Als eines der ersten größeren Projekte wurde das Vorhaben »Corpus Coranicum. Textdokumentation und historisch-litera-

tary.[33] The motives for this initiative were obvious: Why not reconnect scholarship on the Quran to the local Berlin tradition of historical-critical readings of scripture as well as to the Jewish Quran research and try to help it catch up gradually with biblical studies? Pioneering work was required to achieve this. To begin with, the tradition, the Masorah, was to be illuminated, which, in the case of the Quran, has been documented both in writing and orally. The most ancient manuscripts as well as the compendia of the orally transmitted reading variants are to be critically evaluated and made digitally accessible. That which is commonplace elsewhere, namely the critique of the textual tradition and transmission, is for the Quran in this connection not only new but also of great cultural concern, in that the origins of the Quran have been not only geographically but also historically controversial. Only in recent years new discoveries of texts and new techniques of analysis have shown that the Quran, in its present form, with regard to length, to its subdivision into suras and its shape as a consonant text, must have been already fixed around 30 years after the death of Muhammad. The consolidation of the form of the text is thus not indebted first to the imperial politics of the Umayyad Caliph Abd al-Malik ibn Marwān (646–705), but precedes it. – A scholarly literary commentary is to be provided for this text which will include those earlier traditions which have an echo in the Quran and which are now available to us. All this sounds like basic re-

turwissenschaftlicher Kommentar« 2007 an der Berlin-Brandenburgischen Akademie der Wissenschaften initiiert.[33] Die Motive für diese Initiative lagen
auf der Hand: Warum nicht an die lokale Berliner
Tradition der historisch-kritischen Schriftlektüre wie
auch der jüdischen Koranforschung wieder anschlie-
ßen und versuchen, den Vorsprung der Bibelwissen-
schaften gegenüber der Koranwissenschaft allmählich aufzuholen? Dazu war Pionierarbeit gefordert.
Es galt zunächst, die Überlieferung, die Masorah, zu
beleuchten, die im Falle des Koran sowohl schrift-
lich als auch mündlich dokumentiert ist. Es sind also
die ältesten Handschriften ebenso wie die Kompen-
dien der mündlich überlieferten Lesevarianten kritisch zu sichten und digital zugänglich zu machen.
Die anderswo selbstverständliche Überlieferungskri-
tik ist für den Koran in dieser Systematik nicht nur
neu, sie ist auch hochaktuell, denn die Ursprünge des
Koran waren lange nicht nur geographisch, sondern
auch historisch kontrovers. Erst in den letzten Jahren
haben neue Textfunde und neue analytische Tech-
niken erwiesen, dass der Koran in seiner uns vor-
liegenden Textgestalt, was Umfang, Surenuntertei-
lung und Konsonantentext betrifft, bereits zirka 30
Jahre nach dem Tode Muhammads festgelegt haben
muss. Die Fixierung seiner Textform verdankt sich
also nicht erst der imperialen Politik des umayyadi-
schen Kalifen ʿAbdalmalik ibn Marwān (646–705),
sondern geht ihr voraus. Zu diesem Text gilt es nun
unter Einbeziehung der uns inzwischen zuhandenen

search, »Grundlagenforschung«, as is befitting for a project in the academy. Along with this purely academic context, there is, however, another no less relevant secondary context today with regard to the study of early Islam, namely the debate with the institutions for Islamic theology at five German universities which were established almost simultaneously with the project. The founding of these centers of Islamic scholarship, where Muslim teachers pass on their religious tradition and not least the Quran to Muslim students, not only immensely expands the circle of recipients of our research in terms of quantity, it also marks the beginning of a new discursive engagement with the Quran. Its traditional reading will now be drawn into a conversation with the historical-critical approach.

This dialogue is for the time being primarily a program for future exchanges. As is well known, Muslim scholars are said to have reservations about a historical reading of the Quran. Apart from ideological reservations – the handling of the question about the historicity of the Quran by the radical skeptics certainly had a deterrent effect – one could also substantiate reservations with regard to the special relationship between text and commentary in Islam. Thomas Bauer has correctly stressed that the exegetical tradition puts emphasis on the multi-facetedness

Vorgängertraditionen, die im Koran ihr Echo finden, einen literaturwissenschaftlichen Kommentar zu erstellen. Das klingt – wie es sich für ein Akademienvorhaben gehört – nach Grundlagenforschung. Doch gibt es inzwischen für die Beschäftigung mit dem Frühislam einen gegenüber dem rein akademischen nicht minder relevanten zweiten Kontext, nämlich die bereits laufende Debatte mit den fast zeitgleich mit dem Projekt etablierten Islam-Theologien an fünf deutschen Universitäten. Die Einrichtung dieser Zentren islamischer Gelehrsamkeit, an denen muslimische Lehrer ihre Religionstradition und nicht zuletzt den Koran an muslimische Studierende weitergeben, hat nicht nur quantitativ den Rezipientenkreis unserer Forschung immens erweitert, sie markiert überhaupt den Beginn einer neuen, diskursiven Auseinandersetzung mit dem Koran. Seine traditionelle Lektüre wird nun in ein Gespräch mit den historisch-kritischen Lesern hineingezogen.

Dieser Dialog ist vorläufig erst Programm. Es werden muslimischen Forschern bekanntlich oft Vorbehalte gegenüber einer historischen Koranlektüre nachgesagt. Von den ideologischen Vorbehalten abgesehen – gewiss hat der radikal-skeptizistische Umgang mit der Frage der Historizität des Koran eine abschreckende Wirkung gehabt –, könnte man Vorbehalte auch mit dem besonderen Verhältnis zwischen Text und Kommentar im Islam begründen. Thomas Bauer hat zu Recht hervorgehoben, dass die exegetische Tradition auf die Vielgesichtig-

of the Quran, its fundamental »ambiguity«.[34] One of
the earliest genres of commentary which systemati-
cally pursued this approach, the doctrine of the »faces
and aspects,« is transparently named after the standard principle of Jewish biblical exegesis, the discovery of the »faces of the Torah.« Thomas Bauer, who,
however, is aware of the fact that his sensitivity for
the potentials of traditional exegesis is no longer
shared by all modern Muslims, goes so far as to regard the historical reading of the Quran as such as
manipulative and reductive. The ambiguity inherent
to the Quran would be forcefully suppressed by in-
sisting on a single meaning. As much as this would
apply to individual passages with rare lexemes or
Quranic neologisms (his examples are all taken from
the early, mantically influenced suras) – in so far as
these lose much of their effect through the identification with a single meaning while excluding others
which can also be heard in the text – it applies less to
the Quranic echoes of biblical narratives. Prophetic
speech, it is true, lives in large part from its poetic
quality and thus from an openness to different asso-
ciations. In the case with the Quran, however, which
in wide parts is a text of debate, prophetic speech is
equally aimed at a political goal. Its negotiation with
and rectification of established deposits of knowledge, of concepts and doctrines, which are not de-
livered in poetic but discursive text units, very much
requires a »lack of ambiguity«. If one wanted to limit
the Quranic communication to poetic discourse, the

keit des Korans, auf seine prinzipielle Mehrdeutigkeit, großen Wert legt.[34] Eine der frühesten Kommentargattungen, die diesen Zugang systematisch verfolgt, die Lehre von den »Gesichtern und Aspekten«, nennt sich durchsichtig nach dem Standardprinzip jüdischer Bibelexegese, der Auffindung von »Gesichtern der Torah«. Thomas Bauer, der sich allerdings bewusst ist, dass seine Sensitivität gegenüber den Potentialen der traditionellen Exegese längst nicht mehr von allen modernen Muslimen geteilt wird, geht so weit, die historische Lektüre des Korans als solche für manipulativ und reduktiv zu erklären. Die im Koran selbst angelegte Vieldeutigkeit werde durch die Insistenz auf einer einzigen Bedeutung gewaltsam unterdrückt. So sehr dies auch für einzelne Passagen mit seltenen Lexemen oder Wortneuschöpfungen des Koran gelten würde – seine Beispiele sind durchweg den frühen, mantisch geprägten Suren entnommen –, die durch die Identifikation mit einem einzigen Inhalt unter Ausschaltung mit-anklingender anderer viel an Wirkungsmacht verlieren müssen, so wenig trifft es gerade für die koranischen Echos biblischer Erzählungen zu. Prophetische Rede lebt weithin von ihrer Poetizität und damit Offenheit für verschiedene Assoziationen; sie ist im Falle des Korans, der ein Debattentext ist, aber auch auf ein politisches Ziel hin ausgerichtet. Ihre Verhandlung und Rektifizierung von vorfindlichen Wissensbeständen, von Begriffen und Lehrmeinungen, die nicht in poetischen, sondern diskursiven Texteinheiten ausge-

gradual construction of a congregational identity, reflected in the text, could not be explained.

Is the historical research of Holy Scriptures a prerogative of Western theology?

The call for historical research is not something entirely new among Muslim intellectuals. A historicization project, as it is pursued in the *Corpus Coranicum* project, has already been called for as an ideological corrective by several modern Islamic thinkers. Mohammed Arkoun (1928–2010), for example, the Algerian native who worked at the Sorbonne for a long time, insisted on the necessary separation between the prophetic Islam, the *fait coranique*, and that which separated itself from this in a break of tradition, the canonical Islam, the *fait islamique*.[35] In Arkoun's account, the present malaise of Islam results from historical amnesia, concretely, from the negation of the fissure between the phase of prophecy and that of tradition which was solidifying this prophecy. The religious tradition, which was unjustifiably fused with the prophetic proclamation, established a multitude of new religious authorities. Their standing, from the critical perspective of the social scientist Arkoun, was

tragen werden, erfordert sehr wohl Eindeutigkeit. Wollte man die koranische Kommunikation auf poetische Rede eingrenzen, ließe sich die sich im Text abbildende sukzessive Konstruktion einer Gemeindeidentität nicht erklären.

Ist die historische Erforschung von Heiligen Schriften eine Prärogative westlicher Theologie?

Der Ruf nach historischer Forschung ist unter muslimischen Intellektuellen keineswegs etwas ganz Neues. Ein Historisierungsprojekt, wie es im Corpus Coranicum-Projekt verfolgt wird, wurde bereits von mehreren Neudenkern des Islam als ideologisches Korrektiv eingefordert. So hat der aus Algerien stammende, lange an der Sorbonne wirkende Mohammed Arkoun (1928–2010) auf der notwendigen Trennung zwischen dem prophetischen Islam, dem *fait coranique*, und dem durch einen Traditionsbruch von ihm getrennten kanonischen Islam, dem *fait islamique*, insistiert.[35] Für Arkoun ist die heutige Malaise des Islam Resultat einer Geschichtsvergessenheit, konkret der Negierung des Einschnitts zwischen der Phase der Prophetie und der diese Prophetie verfestigenden Überlieferung. Die religiöse Überlieferung, die unberechtigt mit der prophetischen Verkündigung fusioniert wurde, hat eine Vielzahl neuer religiöser Autoritäten etabliert, deren Rang sich (aus

due not to religious but political and social factors which, up to this day, imposed strict limits on free thinking. Arkoun therefore calls for a historicization of the earliest history of Islam; he addresses a breaking of the taboo of that which he calls the »unthought in Islamic thought.« And other new thinkers, such as Nasr Abu Zayd (1943–2010), Muhammad Shabestari and 'Abdalkarim Sorush[36] call for a »historical« reading – without, however, thinking seriously of a contextualization of the Quran with biblical tradition.

But does Arkoun's challenge have a chance to be accepted in the intra-Islamic context? It may be that his appeal did not reach beyond his circles of secularized Muslim intellectuals in his lifetime. Yet his call to separate the Quran from the tradition sounds far more decisive than it actually is. The Quran owes its sacredness not to a semantic alterity in contrast to other late antique text-worlds, but rather to its theological status as *logos*, as an intermediary between the transcendent world of ideas and the earthly world. Its visual coding through its peculiar orthography and calligraphy, as well as its auditory coding through cantilena have given it a place primarily in the area of meditation and prayer. In addition to this it also has a unique status as the verbalized guidance of the community, a status which was crucial during the proclamation. Since the Prophet's death, however, the

der kritischen Perspektive des Sozialwissenschaftlers Arkoun betrachtet) gar nicht religiösen, sondern politisch-sozialen Faktoren verdankt, die aber bis heute dem freien Denken enge Grenzen setzen. Arkoun fordert daher eine Historisierung der frühesten Islamgeschichte, er spricht dabei von einer Enttabuisierung des (von ihm so bezeichneten) »Undenkbaren im islamischen Denken«. Und auch andere Neudenker wie Nasr Hamid Abu Zaid (1943–2010), Muhammad Shabestari und ʿAbdalkarim Sorush[36], fordern eine »historische« Lektüre – ohne dabei allerdings primär an eine Kontextualisierung des Koran mit der biblischen Tradition zu denken.

Hat Arkouns Herausforderung aber Chancen, innerislamisch aufgenommen zu werden? Es mag sein, dass sein Appell zu seinen Lebzeiten nicht über die Kreise säkularisierter Intellektueller hinausgedrungen ist. Doch klingt seine Forderung, den Koran von der Tradition abzusondern, einschneidender als sie ist: Der Koran verdankt seine Sakralität ja nicht einer semantischen Alterität gegenüber anderen spätantiken Textwelten, sondern seinem theologischen Rang als Logos, als Vermittler zwischen der transzendenten Welt der Ideen und der irdischen Welt. Seine visuelle Kodierung durch eine eigene Orthographie und Kalligraphie sowie seine auditive Kodierung durch Kantilene weisen ihm primär einen Platz im Bereich der Meditation und des Gebets zu. Hinzu kommt sein einzigartiger Rang als die verbalisierte Rechtleitung der Gemeinde, den er während der

Quran has shared its normative authority with other authorities, especially with the legal literature which emerged shortly thereafter. Going into the modern period, this legal literature corresponded in its status to that of the Mishna which provides scripture, i.e. the biblical text, with a juridical interpretation.

Where do we stand as critical Quran researchers?

From our outsider perspective we cannot, of course, aspire to interfere in the current processes of the reform of Islam. We can, however, provide an impetus for a more adequate perception of the Quran which does not simply take the fault lines of contemporary intra-Islamic controversies as fixed, but rather keeps them in view as valuable critique. In Islamic studies so far, the almost automatically presented synopsis of the Quran and selected examples from Islamic exegesis – compare, for example, the most recent large project of the *Encyclopedia of the Qur'an*[37] – obstructs the view of the innovative character of the proclamation in the history of religions. To further explicate this innovation remains a scholarly *desideratum*. It is, above all, necessary for our own intellectual discourse today in order to encourage Christian theol-

Verkündigung innehatte. Jedoch vor allem während dieser Verkündigung, denn seine normative Autorität teilt der Koran seit dem Tode des Propheten mit anderen Instanzen, vor allem der sich bald herausbildenden Rechtsliteratur. Sie entsprach bis in die Moderne hinein im Rang etwa der Mischna, die ja ebenfalls der Schrift, das heißt dem biblischen Text, eine juridische Auslegung zur Seite stellt.

Wo stehen wir als kritische Koranforscher?

Uns kann es aus unserer Außenseiterperspektive heraus natürlich nicht um eine Einmischung in die gegenwärtig laufenden Prozesse der Reform des Islam gehen, wohl aber um den Anstoß zu einer angemesseneren Wahrnehmung des Koran, die nicht die gegenwärtigen innerislamischen Verwerfungen einfach festschreibt, sondern sie kritisch im Blick hat. Die bisher in der Islamwissenschaft – man denke an das neueste Großprojekt, die Encyclopedia of the Qur'an[37] – fast automatisch angestellte Synopse von Koran und ausgewählten Beispielen aus der aus ihm erwachsenen islamischen Exegese verstellt die Sicht in die religionsgeschichtliche Innovation der Verkündigung. Diese Innovation herauszuarbeiten, ist immer noch Desiderat. Sie ist heute vor allem für unseren eigenen intellektuellen Diskurs selbst erfor-

ogy to take a (long denied) new look at a sister tradition.

Important impulses have already been provided in this direction in recent years from Christian theologians.[38] A certain fuzziness regarding the Quranic statements nevertheless remains if one reads the Quran as a textual continuum and thus as a static text (as is the usual practice, given that a binding chronology is still not available). What has to be taken into consideration is that during the 22 years of proclamation, important theological positions changed radically. Recognizing these changes and »rectifications« is essential for understanding the Quranic message as a dynamic process. Generally, one can speak of a gradual de-politicization of the biblical traditions; these were politically charged as testimonies of Jewish salvation history but they receive a universal impulse in the Quranic proclamation. An example of this is the Exodus story. In the biblical context, it symbolized paradigmatically the conflict between a prophet and the ruling powers in which the deliverance of the Israelites through the preceding plagues of Egypt takes on the dimension of a threat to the survival of a great empire. In the Quranic versions the incident is presented as the story of the rescue of an individual messenger and those with him, lacking any significant political implications. By contrast, one can also identify a re-politicization of these now neutralized traditions

derlich – um der christlichen Theologie den bisher so
lange verweigerten Blick auf eine Schwestertradition
von neuem nahezulegen.

Dazu sind in den letzten Jahren gerade seitens
christlicher Theologen bereits wichtige Anstöße gegeben worden.[38] Eine gewisse Unschärfe hinsichtlich
der koranischen Aussagen bleibt aber bestehen, wenn
man den Koran als Textkontinuum, wie es angesichts
des noch immer Fehlens einer verbindlichen Chronologie bisher geschieht, und damit als einen statischen
Text liest. Denn es haben sich während der 22 Jahre
andauernden Verkündigung wichtige theologische
Positionen radikal geändert; die Erkenntnis gerade
dieser Wandlungen und »Rektifikationen« ist für ein
Verständnis der koranischen Botschaft als eines dy-
namischen Prozesses unverzichtbar. Generell lässt
sich von einer sukzessiven Entpolitisierung der biblischen Traditionen sprechen, die als Zeugnisse der jüdischen Heilsgeschichte politisch aufgeladen waren,
in der koranischen Verkündigung aber eine universale Stoßrichtung erhalten. So wird etwa die Exo-
dus-Geschichte – die im biblischen Kontext exempla-
risch die Auseinandersetzung zwischen Prophet und
Machthaber versinnbildlicht, wobei die Befreiung
der Israeliten durch die vorausgehenden ägyptischen
Plagen die Dimension der Bestandsgefährdung eines
Großreichs annimmt – in den koranischen Versionen
ohne nennenswerte politische Implikationen als die
Geschichte der Rettung eines individuellen Gesandten und der Seinen erzählt. Gegenläufig lässt sich eine

through which the new people of God, the early community, are integrated into the biblical tradition. An example of this will be presented with the story of Abraham's sacrifice which is transferred to the Meccan context. It is these inversions which can only be recognized through a diachronic reading that are instrumental in the Quran's responding to the ever new challenges and thus constitute the autonomy of the Quran.

The Quran of late antiquity in the field of tension of »scripture, poetry and community formation«

It is not enough, however, to follow the development of the Quranic proclamation solely against the background of the biblical tradition. The Berlin project therefore does not derive the genesis of the Quran, as is currently practiced primarily in the United States, from a single source of inspiration, but from a more complex area of conflict. Here one could speak of a triangle of the three corners of »scripture« (i.e. the biblical tradition), »poetry« (i.e. the linguistic culture of Arabia) and »community formation.« In order to keep the critical and constructive tension between the three corner points together we – together with some avant-garde Arab thinkers – are putting the

Repolitisierung der auf diese Weise neutralisierten Traditionen feststellen, durch die nun das neue Gottesvolk, die frühe Gemeinde, in die biblische Tradition hereingeholt wird. Ein Beispiel dazu wird mit der in den mekkanischen Kontext versetzten Geschichte des Abrahamsopfers vorgestellt werden. Es sind gerade diese nur bei diachroner Lektüre erkennbar werdenden Kehrtwendungen, mit denen auf jeweils neue Herausforderungen geantwortet wird, die die Eigengesetzlichkeit des Koran ausmachen.

Der spätantike Koran im Spannungsfeld »Schrift, Poesie und Gemeindebildung«

Und doch reicht es nicht, die Entwicklung der koranischen Verkündigung einzig vor dem Hintergrund der biblischen Tradition zu verfolgen. Das Berliner Projekt leitet die Genese des Koran daher nicht, wie es gegenwärtig vor allem in den USA geschieht, aus einer einzigen Inspirationsquelle ab, sondern aus einem komplexeren Spannungsfeld. Man könnte von einem Dreieck sprechen, das von den Ecken »Schrift«, das heißt biblische Tradition, »Poesie«, das heißt sprachliche Kultur Arabiens, und »Gemeindebildung« abgesteckt wird. Um dieses Spannungsfeld zusammenzuhalten, stellen wir – gemeinsam mit einigen avantgardistischen arabischen Denkern – den

Quran in the wider horizon of late antiquity. This step is new and not entirely uncontroversial.[39]

That the concept of »late antiquity« has not yet caught on in the research of Islamic studies cannot be overlooked. The Quran and early Islam are here traditionally seen as the starting point of an autochthonous »Islamic culture.« Geiger's revolutionary relocalization of the Quran in late antiquity is mostly forgotten. If taken seriously, it could indeed irritate the self-definition of the subject area of Islamic studies. Such fears of loss do not concern historians critical of Orientalism in Oriental studies like Aziz Al-Azmeh who is one of the few contemporary scholars of Islam who represents the belief that:

[…] Paleo-Muslim religion and polity are intelligible only in terms of conditions and structures that mark the broader history of Late Antiquity. […] By placing it in the context of late antiquity it becomes possible to counter-act the tendency to construe a perspective on the genesis of Islam without the all-too-common recourse to contrastive histories of East and West, or the equally common presumption that Islam was somehow frozen in a perpetual moment of inception […].[40]

Certainly, the term »late antiquity« is an eminently European epochal term which seems to presuppose the idea of Greek antiquity as the golden age and evoke the conventional Euro-centric outline of epochs, according to which antiquity is followed by the »middle ages« and they, in turn, by the »renais-

Koran in den weiteren Horizont der Spätantike. Dieser Schritt ist neu und nicht ganz unkontrovers.[39]

Denn es ist nicht zu übersehen, dass sich das Konzept »Spätantike« in der islamwissenschaftlichen Forschung noch nicht durchgesetzt hat. Der Koran und frühe Islam werden hier traditionell als Anfangspunkt einer autochthonen »islamischen Kultur« begriffen. Geigers revolutionäre Relokalisierung des Koran in die Spätantike ist zumeist vergessen; sie würde vielleicht auch – wirklich ernstgenommen – an der Selbstdefinition des Faches Islamwissenschaft rütteln. Solche Verlustängste berühren allerdings orientalistikkritische Historiker wie Aziz Al-Azmeh nicht, der als einer der wenigen zeitgenössischen Islamwissenschaftler die Überzeugung vertritt, dass

> [...] die Paleo-Muslimische Religion und Politik nur denkbar sind im Rahmen der Bedingungen und Strukturen, die die weitere Geschichte der Spätantike bestimmen. [...] Mit der Einordnung in die Spätantike lässt sich der nur allzu geläufigen Konstruktion von kontrastiven Geschichten in Ost und West, wie auch der ebenso üblichen Annahme entgegenwirken, im Islam sei Geschichte gewissermaßen in ihrer Anfangssituation stillgestellt. [...].[40]

Gewiss, »Spätantike« ist ein eminent europäischer Epochenbegriff, der die Vorstellung von der griechischen Antike als Goldenem Zeitalter vorauszusetzen scheint und die konventionelle – eurozentrische – Epochengliederung evoziert, der zufolge auf die Antike das »Mittelalter« und auf dieses eine »Renais-

sance« which rediscovered antiquity. The actual »inventor« of the late antiquity discourse which is so lively today, the historian Peter Brown, who lets late antiquity continue to 750, could not, to a serious degree, integrate Islam into this era. Indeed, in purely chronological terms the proclamation of the Quran between 610 and 632 would still fall within late antiquity as he delineated it. In early Islam, however, Brown does not recognize a manifestation of the thought of late antiquity but an indigenous Arab culture which could be integrated for a limited period in the world of late antiquity only because of its assimilation to Christianity. In Brown's reading, the proclamation of Muhammad is not associated with the process of a community formation on the basis of a cross-religious communal education, but rather with a foreign import:

It was a stroke of genius on the part of Muhammad to turn this essentially foreign message into a principle on the basis of which the conflict-ridden society of the Hijaz could reorganize itself.[41]

What then of Islam as a substantially new epoch, as an absolute beginning? This comes close to the traditional Islamic perception which not least Arab intellectuals, such as the Lebanese historian Samir Kassir, have challenged. For the overcoming of the »Arab malaise« in the twenty-first century, he calls for a radical historicization of the events and for a history »without religious predestination or nationalistic tel-

sance« folgt, in der die Antike wiederentdeckt wird. Der eigentliche »Erfinder« des heute so lebendigen Spätantike-Diskurses, der Historiker Peter Brown, der die Spätantike bis 750 andauern lässt, hat daher auch mit der Integration des Islam in diese Epoche nicht recht ernstmachen können. Denn rein chronologisch betrachtet müsste die Verkündigung des Koran zwischen 610 und 632 noch in die von ihm abgesteckte Spätantike fallen. Brown erkennt im frühen Islam aber keine Manifestation spätantiken Denkens, sondern eine autochthone arabische Kultur, die sich nur dank ihrer Assimilation an die Christen für eine begrenzte Frist in die Welt der Spätantike integrieren konnte. Er assoziiert mit der Verkündigung Muhammads nicht den Prozess einer Gemeindebildung auf der Basis einer religionenübergreifenden Bildung, sondern einen fremdländischen Import:

Es war ein Geniestreich Mohammeds, diese im wesentlichen fremde Botschaft zu einem Prinzip zu machen, nach dem sich die von Konflikten geschüttelte Gesellschaft des Hedjaz selbst reorganisieren konnte.[41]

Der Islam als eine substantiell neue Epoche, als ein absoluter Anfang? Dies ist auch die traditionell islamische Wahrnehmung, der nicht zuletzt arabische Intellektuelle wie der libanesische Historiker Samir Kassir entgegengetreten sind. Er plädiert zur Überwindung des »arabischen Unglücks« im 21. Jahrhundert für eine radikale Historisierung der Ereignisse und spricht sich für eine Geschichtsschreibung »ohne

eology.« Although the term »late antiquity« is not used explicitly, he emphasizes the enduring character of the dynamics from late antiquity:

> Religious predestination clearly shapes the canonical version, which holds that the history of the Arabs starts with the revelation of the Quran, and skirts over everything before as a time of chaos, or *Djahiliyya* (the age of ignorance or barbarism). [...] Yet this chaotic image does not fit with recent Roman and Hellenistic historical scholarship about the Arabian Peninsula. [...] we can only imagine the Copernican revolution that would be brought about by the discovery of a golden age that preceded the alleged golden age.[42]

Kassir laments that the dominant conception of history in Arab academia also follows the standard European three-step model of history which is merely extended to the Arab world. The golden age which was initiated by the Prophet is followed by a long period of decline, which is called either the »middle ages« or the »age of decline« (*'asr al-inḥiṭāṭ*). A renaissance (*nahḍa*) then follows at the end of the 19th century. Since this is, however, now widely regarded as a failure, the golden age, according to this idea, flows into an endlessly continuing decline – a self-perception of modern Arab intellectuals in which Kassir sees the »Arab malaise.«

religiöse Vorherbestimmung oder nationalistische Teleologie« aus. Ohne den Begriff »Spätantike« explizit zu verwenden, hebt er die Nachhaltigkeit spätantiker Dynamiken hervor:

> Die kanonische Sichtweise zeigt das Wirken der religiösen Vorherbestimmung: Sie lässt arabische Geschichte mit der koranischen Offenbarung beginnen und behält von den vorhergehenden Zeiten nur ein chaotisches Bild zurück, das sich in dem Begriff *Djahiliyya* (Zeitalter des Unwissens bzw. der Barbarei) verdichtet. [...] Dieses chaotische Bild lässt sich jedoch nicht aufrechterhalten, wenn man neuere Forschungsergebnisse über die hellenistische und römische Geschichte der Halbinsel berücksichtigt [...]; man kann sich ausmalen, welche kopernikanische Wende die Anerkennung eines Goldenen Zeitalters auslösen müsste, das dem vermeintlichen Goldenen Zeitalter vorausgegangen wäre.[42]

Auch die in der arabischen Akademia herrschende Geschichtsauffassung folgt, wie Kassir beklagt, dem für die europäische Geschichte typischen Dreischritt-Modell, das lediglich in die arabische Welt verlegt wird. Einem vom Propheten herbeigeführten Goldenen Zeitalter folgt eine lange Verfallsperiode, die entweder »Mittelalter« oder auch »Niedergangszeit« (*'aṣr al-inḥiṭāṭ*) genannt wird. Eine Renaissance (*nahḍa*) erfolgt dann zu Ende des 19. Jahrhunderts. Da diese jedoch heute in weiten Kreisen als gescheitert betrachtet wird, mündet das Goldene Zeitalter dieser Vorstellung zufolge in einen endlos fortdauernden Verfall ein – eine Selbstsicht moderner arabischer

The Quran as an active player in the intellectual context of late antiquity

The objective of the Berlin project is to redefine the term »late antiquity« – a term that has not yet attained acceptance in the Arab world. It is to be understood not as an epoch but as an intellectual space (Denkraum). Here the focus is put on the hermeneutical new readings of canonical texts and exegetical textual strategies. Debates from late antiquity are here understood as »later re-readings« of canonical traditions of »antiquity.«[43]

In the case of the Quran, this is not a matter of contemporaneity alone but a matter of its status as an active player in the »intellectual context of late antiquity.« Let's have another look at the triangular field of tension: »scripture, poetry, that is, Arabic linguistic culture, and community formation.« The Quran is an active player in so far as it »biblicizes« an extant secular worldview and in this way, as we shall see, constructs a counter-history for the Arabian Peninsula. The significance of this breakthrough is difficult to overestimate. Indeed, the biblical tradition and the ancient Arabic poetry were initially two powerful but – in terms of their ethos – rival canons. In the local Bedouin-imprinted Arab culture, tribal values

Intellektueller, in der Kassir »das Unglück der Araber« sieht.

Der Koran als *active player* im Denkraum Spätantike

Ziel des Berliner Projektes ist es nun, den – bis jetzt im arabischen Raum noch nicht durchgedrungenen – Begriff »Spätantike« neu zu definieren: nicht mehr als eine Epoche, sondern als einen *Denkraum*, in dem es um hermeneutische Neulektüren kanonischer Texte und um exegetische Textstrategien geht. Spätantike Debatten werden hier als »spätere Relektüren« von »antiken«, kanonischen Traditionen verstanden.[43]

Beim Koran darf es dabei aber nicht um bloße Zeitgenossenschaft gehen, sondern um seinen Status als *active player* im »Denkraum Spätantike«. Werfen wir noch einmal einen Blick auf das trigonale Spannungsfeld »Schrift – Poesie (das heißt arabische sprachliche Kultur) – Gemeindebildung«. *Active player* ist der Koran insofern, als er eine vorgefundene säkulare Weltanschauung »biblisiert«, dass er dabei, wie wir sehen werden, sogar eine Gegengeschichte für die arabische Halbinsel konstruiert. Dieser Durchbruch ist kaum zu überschätzen. Denn mit der biblischen Tradition und der altarabischen Poesie standen sich zunächst zwei mächtige, hinsichtlich ihres Ethos aber rivalisierende Canones gegenüber.

ranked high in the value system.[44] They permitted the tribal elite a heroic self-realization and allowed them to live out their passions excessively. Restraint, prudence, *ḥilm*, analogous to the Greek *sophrosyne*, was indeed an acknowledged virtue, but it was the opposite that counted no less among the prerogatives of the Bedouin elite, *djahl*, licentiousness, limitless waste in hospitality and death-defying engagement in battle. It was only through their own excesses that the Beduin pagans were able to rise above the powers of fate which governed their lives.[45] The ethos carried by the biblical tradition, in which the human being was understood to be a »servant of God« – no longer autonomous but »loyal« and »faithful« – could not have been further from the Bedouin ethos.

Scripture and poetry

Together with this ethos, it was above all the view of the world which was transformed through the Quran, in that it now received an eschatological dimension. According to the early Quran, the world provides a sign system that refers back to the archetypal heavenly scripture of all prophetic revelations. With the elevation of scripture to the highest authority, there is a practical transition from a culture that is only rudimentarily scriptural to a culture that is

In der beduinisch geprägten arabischen Lokalkultur standen tribale Werte hoch in der Rangordnung,[44] sie erlaubten einer Stammeselite heroische Selbstverwirklichung und ein exzessives Ausleben ihrer Leidenschaften. Zurückhaltung, Besonnenheit, *ḥilm* (entsprechend der griechischen *sophrosyne*) war zwar eine anerkannte Tugend, doch zählte das Gegenteil, *djahl*, Zügellosigkeit, grenzenlose Verschwendung in der Gastfreundschaft, und todesmutiger Einsatz im Kampf, mindestens ebenso zu den Prärogativen der beduinischen Elite, die sich nur durch eigene Exzesse über die Schicksalsmächte erheben konnte, denen sie sich preisgegeben wusste.[45] Das von der biblischen Tradition getragene Ethos, in dem der Mensch als »Diener Gottes« nicht mehr autonom, sondern »ergeben« sein sollte, hätte nicht weiter von dem vorgefundenen Beduinenethos entfernt sein können.

Schrift und Poesie

Zusammen mit dem Ethos wandelte sich durch den Koran aber vor allem auch die Sicht auf die Welt, die nun eine eschatologische Dimension erhielt. Die Welt bietet bereits dem frühen Koran zufolge ein Zeichensystem, das rückverweist auf die himmlische Urschrift aller prophetischen Offenbarungen. Mit der Erhebung der Schrift zur höchsten Autorität vollzieht sich praktisch der Wechsel von einer nur rudimentär schriftlichen Kultur in eine schrift-

scripturally oriented. In the categories of Jan Assmann, the ritual coherence of society makes space
for textual coherence.[46] This did not happen because
scripture would have been new on the horizon of
the Arabs but rather because of the newly established
high authority of writing as an earthly image of
scripture in heaven.[47] It is only logical that with the
Quran, for the first time, a written Arabic »text« appears which was worthy of the term. From the time
before this, with regard to written documents, we
only have short inscriptions.[48] Of course, this should
not hide the fact that the orally communicated and
linguistically as well as rhetorically highly developed
poetry for a broad public laid the foundation for its
cultural identity, insofar as it authenticated the purity
of the high Arabic language which was maintained
by all Arab tribes as a unifying medium.[49] Only on
this basis could the Quran prevail as an authoritative
text: it was the social meaning of the poetic language established in poetry that provided the prere-
quisite for the reception of the largely poetic Quran.
Notwithstanding the importance of poetry for the
emergence and penetrating power of the Quran, in
contemporary scholarship the linguistic embeddedness of the Quran is completely sidelined.

What made the community of the Prophet a community with an identity of its own was triggered

lich orientierte; in den Kategorien von Jan Assmann gesprochen macht rituelle Kohärenz der Gesellschaft textueller Kohärenz Platz.[46] Dies geschieht nicht, weil etwa Schrift neu in den Horizont der Araber getreten wäre, sondern einzig aufgrund der neu etablierten hohen Autorität von Schrift als eines irdischen Abbilds der himmlischen Schrift.[47] Es ist nur konsequent, dass mit dem Koran zum ersten Mal ein geschriebener arabischer Text, der dieser Beschreibung wert ist, in Erscheinung tritt. Aus der Zeit vorher besitzen wir an schriftlichen Dokumenten nur kurze Inschriftentexte.[48] Natürlich darf dieser Stand der Dinge nicht darüber hinwegtäuschen, dass die mündlich überlieferte, sprachlich und rhetorisch hochentwickelte Dichtung einer breiten Öffentlichkeit die Basis für ihre kulturelle Identität gelegt hatte, insofern sie die Reinheit der von allen arabischen Stämmen als verbindendes Medium gepflegten arabischen Hochsprache verbürgte.[49] Erst auf dieser Grundlage konnte sich der Koran als autoritativer Text durchsetzen, wobei die von der Dichtung etablierte soziale Bedeutung poetischer Sprache erst die Vorbedingung für die Rezeption des seinerseits weitgehend poetischen Koran lieferte. Ungeachtet der Bedeutung der Dichtung für die Entstehung und Durchschlagskraft des Koran steht die sprachliche Einbettung des Koran in der gegenwärtigen Forschung im Schatten des Interesses.

Was die Gemeinde des Propheten aber erst zu einer neuen Identitätsgemeinschaft machte, war die

by the Quran's »enchantment of the world.« The Prophet was repeatedly accused of »word magic« by his opponents – a transformation of the empirical world into a self-transcending symbolic world. As much as this biblical reading of the world (as a creation pointing to the *eschaton*) encountered resistance during the genesis of the Quran itself, in the end it prevailed. This Quranic »enchanted world,« as much as it was biblically influenced, should not simply be understood as a »third shoot« of the Hebrew Bible (after the Jewish and Christian tradition) which established itself next to the Jewish and Christian world of faith. For Arabic thought not only »biblicized« itself, it also conversely »arabicized« biblical thought. A new *topographia sacra* emerged with Mecca as the new Jerusalem. Above all, instead of Moses, who had stood in the foreground for a long time, the pre-Mosaic man of God, Abraham, becomes the founder of the newly emerging tradition and his genealogical relationship to Arabia becomes newly virulent. With the emphasis being placed on the biblical precedents of the Quran, this development has remained largely unnoticed in contemporary research.

vom Koran ausgelöste »Verzauberung der Welt«. Dem Propheten wird von seinen Gegnern immer wieder »Wortzauber« vorgeworfen – eine Verwandlung der Welt in eine über sich selbst hinausweisende Zeichenwelt. So sehr diese biblische Lesung der Welt (als eines auf das Eschaton verweisenden Schöpfungstextes) während der Korangenese selbst aber auch auf Widerstand stieß – sie hat sich, wie das schließliche Durchdringen des Islam beweist, am Ende behauptet. Diese koranisch »verzauberte Welt«, so sehr sie auch biblisch geprägt ist, ist dabei nicht einfach als ein nach der jüdischen und christlichen Tradition »dritter Spross« der hebräischen Bibel zu verstehen, der sich neben die jüdische und die christliche Glaubenswelt stellt. Denn nicht nur biblisiert sich das arabische Denken, es arabisiert umgekehrt auch das biblische Denken. Es entsteht eine neue Topographia sacra mit Mekka als neuem Jerusalem, auch und vor allem wird aber anstelle des lange Zeit im Vordergrund stehenden Mose der vor-mosaische Gottesmann Abraham, dessen genealogische Beziehungen zu Arabien nun virulent werden, zum eigentlichen Stifter der sich neu herausbildenden Tradition – eine Entwicklung, die angesichts der exklusiven Schwerpunktsetzung auf den biblischen Präzendenzen des Koran in der gegenwärtigen Forschung weitestgehend ausgeblendet bleibt.

Community formation

The negotiations that were necessary for biblicizing the Arab world view in the first place and then later fusing the new worldview with the local Arab traditions are reflected in the debates of the later Meccan and Medinan suras. In terms of genre these suras do not have any equivalent in the earlier traditions either in narrative or homiletics, but are rather much closer to »drama.« Indeed, the assertion of a new truth of faith could not have taken place without involving the audience of the proclamation. In order to ensure the continuation of the process of proclamation, the texts always had to achieve a consensus with these communication partners.

This third pivotal point in the three-pole scheme, »scripture, poetry and community formation,« is completely absent in Western Quran research today. A still rampant epistemic pessimism has it that even the assumption that Muhammad actually preached to listeners appears as speculation. The social embeddedness, the *Sitz im Leben* (social setting in life), of an individual Quranic text had been a major concern not only for previous generations of Western scholarship, but also for the Islamic tradition. Not only Theodor Nöldeke, who, in 1860, published for the first time his groundbreaking *History of the Quran*[50] but muslim scholars long before him, in the tenth century, had distinguished between Meccan and

Gemeindebildung

Die Verhandlungen, die dazu nötig waren, zunächst das arabische Weltbild zu biblisieren und später das neue Weltbild mit den lokalen arabischen Traditionen zu verflechten, spiegeln sich in den Debatten der späteren mekkanischen und dann der medinischen Suren, die gattungsmäßig in den früheren Traditionen weder narrativ noch homiletisch eine Entsprechung haben, sondern die vielmehr dem »Drama« am nächsten stehen. Denn die Durchsetzung einer neuen Glaubenswahrheit konnte sich nicht an der Hörerschaft der Verkündigung vorbei vollziehen, sie musste – um den Fortgang des Verkündigungsprozesses zu gewährleisten – immer wieder den Konsens dieser Kommunikationspartner finden.

Der damit benannte dritte Angelpunkt in dem dreipoligen Schema »Schrift – Poesie – Gemeindebildung« wird in der westlichen Koranforschung heute vollständig ausgeblendet. Ein noch immer grassierender epistemischer Pessimismus lässt bereits die Annahme einer historischen Verkündigung Muhammads an Hörer spekulativ erscheinen. Die soziale Einbettung, der Sitz im Leben eines einzelnen Korantextes hatte dagegen nicht nur die früheren westlichen Forscher, sondern auch die islamische Tradition beschäftigt. Nicht erst Theodor Nöldeke, der 1860 erstmals seine bahnbrechende »Geschichte des Qorans«[50] vorlegte, sondern bereits muslimische Gelehrte des 10. Jahrhunderts haben zwischen mek-

Medinan suras. In a specific genre of commentary, the *asbāb al-nuzūl*, the »occasions of the revelation,«[51] individual pronouncements are even embedded in an individual social situation, and, not infrequently, a plurality of actors are presented as involved in the genesis of the respective proclamation.

The Berlin historical-critical project has gone one step further by reading the text itself as an essentially linear proclamation that eventually arrives at its goal – the achievement of a religious identity of the listeners as a community. Muhammad may indeed be considered a teacher of late antiquity who – as John of Damascus put it – called forth a *hairesis*, which originally meant »school.« Later observers from the Eastern Church preserved this image in calling the Quran a teaching and not a book.[52] »Linear,« however, does not have to mean »straight.« The suras show traces of often repeated recitation whereby new insights could be added time and time again. One might compare here the Targums of the early Jewish tradition, though the difference is that in the case of the Quran the new interpretations do not appear next to the text, but are brought right into the process of the text's construction. Not infrequently it was the biblical stories which made an expansion of the text necessary since their full theological dimension could only come to light after repeated recitation (possibly provoked by listeners who were versant in the biblical tradition). Almost all Meccan

kanischen und medinischen Suren unterschieden. In einer eigenen Kommentargattung, den *asbāb al-nuzūl* (»Anlässe der Offenbarung«),[51] bettet man die einzelnen Verkündigungen sogar in eine individuelle soziale Situation ein und beteiligt nicht selten eine Mehrzahl von Akteuren an der Genese der betreffenden Verkündigung.

Das Berliner historisch-kritische Projekt geht nun noch einen entscheidenden Schritt weiter und liest den Text selbst als eine im wesentlichen lineare Verkündigung, die schließlich an einem Ziel – der Erreichung einer religiösen Identität der Hörer als Gemeinde – ankommt. Muhammad kann ja als ein spätantiker Lehrer gelten, der (wie Johannes von Damaskus es ausdrückt) eine *hairesis*, was ja zunächst einmal eine »Schule« meint, ins Leben gerufen hat – ein Bild, das spätere ostkirchliche Beobachter, die den Koran nicht als Buch, sondern als Lehre behandeln, bewahrt haben.[52] »Linear« muss dabei nicht »zielgerade« bedeuten; die Suren zeigen Spuren einer oft wiederholten Rezitation, wobei immer wieder neue Einsichten nachgetragen werden konnten, vergleichbar den Targumen der frühen jüdischen Tradition, nur dass die Neudeutungen im Fall des Koran nicht neben den Text treten, sondern gleich in den sich konstituierenden Text aufgenommen werden. Nicht selten sind es biblische Geschichten, deren volle theologische Dimension erst bei wiederholter Rezitation, eventuell herausgefordert durch neu hinzugekommene in der biblischen Tradition diskur-

suras exhibit these kinds of »supplements.« One could therefore describe the proclamation as a movement of exchange between different communication partners, a typical characteristic of schools. What changes in the course of development is not – as would be the case, for example, in the fictional work of secular writers – the stance of the »author« or the message itself. What changes are the listeners who, over time, are recruited from ever more heterogeneous groups and who, in the course of their »education,« come to new insights. The proclamation responds to their changing expectations. During the proclamation, it is therefore not only texts that extend the established stock of biblical knowledge and explore their meaning, but above all the practioners of biblical tradition entering into the debate.

II
How does scripture come to be?

After this detailed analysis of the emergence of the images of the Quran and the manifestations in which the Quran encounters us today in the East and in the West, I wish to turn in the second half of my remarks to the historical genesis of the Quran. The Quran represents a transfer of knowledge of late-an-

siv gebildete Hörer, zutage trat und eine Erweiterung notwendig machte. Fast alle mekkanischen Suren weisen solche »Nachträge« auf. Man könnte also bei der Verkündigung von einer für Schulen charakteristischen Austauschbewegung zwischen verschiedenen Kommunikationspartnern sprechen. Was sich im Laufe der Entwicklung verändert, ist also nicht – wie es etwa in dem Werk profaner Schriftsteller der Fall wäre – die Haltung des »Autors« noch auch die Botschaft selbst, was sich verändert, sind die Hörer, die sich im Laufe der Zeit aus immer heterogeneren Gruppen rekrutieren und die im Verlauf ihrer »Erziehung« zu neuen Einsichten gelangen; auf deren sich wandelnde Erwartungen geht die Verkündigung ein. Es sind also während der Verkündigung nicht etwa nur Texte, die die biblischen Wissensbestände erweitern und in ihrem Sinn ausloten, sondern vor allem die in die Debatte eintretenden Träger biblischer Bildung.

II
Wie entsteht eine Schrift?

Nach diesem ausführlichen Verfolg der Entstehung der Koranbilder, der Manifestationen, in denen uns der Koran heute in Ost und West begegnet, wollen wir uns im zweiten Teil dieser Ausführungen der historischen Korangenese zuwenden. Der Koran spiegelt einen – über die von Geiger beschworene »Auf-

tique traditions. This transfer went far beyond a »reception of Judaism« (as invoked by Geiger) and was above all reciprocal, progressive and regressive. The Quranic proclamation connects the listener to a new biblical-Arabic double narrative. First of all, it breaks apart their locally inherited tribal self-understanding through the foundation of new biblically based ties. It initiates, to a certain degree, a biblicization of Arabic thought. This process is perhaps not unusual in the context of a mission among pagans. The fact that the pendulum swings back again so that, especially at a later stage, and arabicization of biblical ideas can be identified, would also be nothing special in comparisons of religions. What stands out, however, is that both processes are indebted to a new hermeneutics, one that was apparently new for Arabia, namely the form of thinking in terms of typology. This was a characteristic form of the handling of texts in late antiquity. »Typology« – which has already been alluded to as a dimension underlying the narrative style of the Hebrew Bible – shall be, in the following, understood as a collective term for various deliberately employed textual strategies.[53] »Typology in a broad sense,« as the linking up of one's own experiences and practices with older canonical examples, can already be identified in the earliest suras. These can be understood as re-productions, as a new staging of psalmodic presentations. »Typology in the narrower sense,« the positing of analogies between contemporary figures and biblical ones, such as Muhammad and Mo-

nahme aus dem Judentum« weit hinausgehenden, vor allem aber reziproken, vor- und rückläufigen – Wissenstransfer spätantiker Traditionen. Die koranische Verkündigung bindet die Hörer in eine neue biblisch-arabische Doppelnarrative ein: Er sprengt zunächst ihr lokal ererbtes tribales Selbstverständnis durch die Stiftung neuer, biblisch begründeter Bindungen, stößt gewissermaßen eine Biblisierung arabischen Denkens an – einen Prozess, der vielleicht im Kontext der Mission von Paganen noch nichts Ungewöhnliches darstellt. Auch die Tatsache, dass das Pendel wieder zurückschlägt, dass sich, vor allem in einer späteren Phase, eine Arabisierung biblischer Vorstellungen abzeichnet, wäre im Religionsvergleich noch nichts Besonderes. Was hier jedoch auffällt, ist, dass beide Prozesse sich einer für Arabien offenbar neuen Hermeneutik verdanken, nämlich der für den spätantiken Umgang mit Texten charakteristischen Denkform der Typologie. »Typologie«, von der vorher schon als der Erzählweise der Hebräischen Bibel unterschwellig zugrundeliegend die Rede war, wird im Folgenden als Sammelbegriff für verschiedene bewusst eingesetzte Textstrategien[53] verstanden. »Typologie in einem weiten Sinne« als Rückkoppelung eigener Erfahrungen und Praktiken an ältere kanonische Vorbilder zeigt sich bereits in den frühesten Suren, die als Reinszenierungen psalmodierender Vorträge verstanden werden können. »Typologie im engeren Sinne« der Analogsetzung von zeitgenössischen mit biblischen Figuren, etwa Muhammads mit

ses, characterizes the middle Meccan suras. History is here brought into the present, which therefore receives a new theological dimension as part of the divine plan of salvation. A biblically inspired counter-history to the local tradition is thereby successively written – a counter-history not without its dangers since it resulted in deep social crisis and a split in Meccan society. This development required a new strategy to pacify urban society by showing the common bond, indeed the interweaving of Biblical and local traditions. It was achieved through a third, more complex »theologically charged« form of typology: the familiar figure of »promise and fulfillment«, well known from the Jewish and Christian tradition. It is connected especially with Abraham, the bearer of biblical promises *par excellence*, who invoked in a prayer promises of blessing – also for his offspring settling in Arabia. In this way, Mecca becomes an Arabian promised land.

Yet this connection raises new questions which have to do especially with issues relating to cultic practice, such as the Meccan *ḥajj*-rites. How could these still clearly pagan-shaped cultic acts be fit into the biblical worldview? The breakthrough of the community to achieve its own biblical-Arab identity required a still more intense form of typology. This was »mythopoiesis«, the discovery of »primal scenes« related in the Bible which seem to underlie the local

Mose, charakterisiert dann die mittelmekkanischen Suren. Geschichte wird hier in die Gegenwart hereingeholt, die damit eine neue theologische Dimension als Teil des göttlichen Heilsplans erhält. Es wird so sukzessiv eine biblisch inspirierte Gegengeschichte zur Lokaltradition geschrieben, die nicht ungefährlich ist, indem sie die mekkanische Gesellschaft spaltet und eine Krise heraufbeschwört. – Für die sich daher zur Befriedung der Stadtgesellschaft stellende Aufgabe, die Zusammengehörigkeit, ja Verflochtenheit der biblischen und der lokalen Tradition zu erweisen, wird schließlich eine noch komplexere, nämlich »theologisch aufgeladene« Form der Typologie erforderlich: die aus der jüdischen und christlichen Tradition vertraute Denkfigur von Verheißung und Erfüllung. Sie verbindet sich vor allem mit Abraham, dem Träger biblischer Verheißungen par excellence, der in einem Gebet Segensverheißungen auch für seine in Arabien siedelnden Nachkommen erfleht. Mekka wird auf diese Weise zu einem arabischen Gelobten Land.

Doch reißt diese Verbindung neue Fragen auf, die insbesondere Kultisches, die mekkanischen ḥadjdj-Riten, betreffen. Wie lassen sich diese deutlich noch pagan geprägten Kulthandlungen in das biblische Weltbild einordnen? Der Durchbruch der Gemeinde zu einer eigenen, biblisch-arabischen Identität ist nicht ohne eine noch intensivere Form von Typologie ausgekommen, nämlich der Aufdeckung von biblisch gestalteten »Urszenen«, die den loka-

forms of religious practice and which – once discovered – import on them a salvation-historical dimension. One such primal scene is Abraham's sacrifice. This was identified as living forth in the local cultic practice of pilgrimage sacrifice. We shall follow the Quranic engagement with the biblical traditions through these four stages, the first characterized liturgically, the second narratively, the third historically and the fourth mytho-poetically.

Psalm recitation as new liturgical poetry

To start with, we shall focus on the historical beginning: the Quran recitation as »new poetry.« In the context in which the Quran was born, poetry was held to be the highest form of artistic expression. Indeed, it was put vaguely into connection with supernatural powers, although the poet was nevertheless largely free regarding his objective sources of inspiration. While he was religiously unbound, he did have obligations to social and poetic conventions, but not to a single authoritative source of the proclamation of truth. His freedom was limited rather by a deep pessimism, by the agonizing recognition of the *aporia* of history, which posed its riddles in the local ruins of fallen monuments, and refused to allow an end to the oppressive awareness of transitoriness.[54]

len kultischen Verrichtungen zu unterliegen scheinen und die – einmal entdeckt – ihnen eine neue,
heilsgeschichtliche Dimension verleihen. Eine solche
Urszene ist das Abrahamsopfer, das man in der lokalen kultischen Praxis des Opfers bei der Wallfahrt
weiterwirken sieht. – Wir wollen die koranische
Auseinandersetzung mit den biblischen Traditionen
durch die genannten vier Etappen verfolgen, deren
erste liturgisch, die zweite narrativ, die dritte historisch und die vierte mythopoietisch geprägt ist.

Psalm-Rezitation als neue liturgische Poesie

Fokussieren wir zunächst den historischen Anfang:
die Koranrezitation als »neue Poesie«. Denn in der
Landschaft, in die der Koran hineingeboren wurde,
galt die Dichtung als die höchste Form künstlerischen
Ausdrucks, Dichtung wurde zwar vage mit über-
natürlichen Kräften in Verbindung gebracht, doch
stand der Dichter seinen gegenständlichen Inspira-
tionsquellen weithin frei gegenüber. Religiös unge-
bunden war er zwar gesellschaftlichen und auch poetischen Konventionen verpflichtet, nicht aber einer
einzigen autoritativen Quelle der Wahrheitsverkün-
digung. Eingeschränkt war seine Freiheit eher durch
einen tiefen Pessimismus, durch die quälende Wahrnehmung der Aporie gegenüber der Geschichte, deren in Ruinen liegende Monumente Rätsel aufgaben

The Quranic proclamation – which was, quite differently, committed from the outset to a single source of inspiration – takes this as its vantage point. It counters the poetic melancholy in that it overcomes the transitoriness of human life through the eschatologically determined time of God's creation; it releases the ruined places from their historical opacity and – by re-interpreting them as memorials of divine visitations – transfers them into the illuminated space of salvation history.[55] Fate-guided cyclical time is overcome by »linear« time which follows the straight path of divine guidance.[56] Despite its inverted perspective, the Quranic speech nevertheless remains – through the common medium of poetry – typologically connected to the ancient Arab tradition of art. The sura has justly been understood as the »religious ode«, the religious *Qasida*. Typology works connectively: as poem-like presentations the early suras could draw upon the authority of the most prominent form of Arab public speech. It is not surprising that the Messenger of the Quran was repeatedly held to be a poet – a designation which he vehemently opposed, not only to distance himself from the lesser demons (which were associated with poetry), but also to assert his »monism of inspiration«, that is, the divine monopoly to function as a source of legitimate enthusiasms. Poetic practice, which for the earliest listeners meant psalmodic recitation of those

und das beklemmende Bewusstsein der Vergänglichkeit nicht zur Ruhe kommen ließen.[54]

Die koranische Verkündigung, die, ganz anders,
von vornherein einer einzigen Inspirationsquelle verpflichtet ist, setzt hier an. Sie tritt der dichterischen
Melancholie entgegen, indem sie die Vergänglichkeit
des Menschen in der eschatologisch determinierten
Schöpfungszeit Gottes aufhebt und indem sie die
Ruinenstätten aus dem historischen Dunkel heraus
als Erinnerungsorte göttlicher Heimsuchung in den
erhellten Raum der Heilsgeschichte rückt.[55] Schick-
salsgelenkte zyklische Zeit wird durch eine dem ge-
raden Weg göttlicher Leitung folgende »lineare« Zeit
überwunden.[56] Trotz ihrer umgekehrten Perspektive bleibt die koranische Rede aber durch das gemeinsame Medium der Poesie typologisch der altarabischen Kunsttradition verbunden, zu Recht hat man
von der Sure als der religiösen Ode, der religiösen
Qasida, gesprochen. Typologie wirkt konnektiv: Als
gedichtähnliche Vorträge konnten die frühen Suren
von der Autorität der prominentesten Form arabischer öffentlicher Rede zehren. Nicht verwunderlich
ist auch, dass der Verkünder des Koran wiederholt als
Dichter wahrgenommen wurde – eine Zuordnung,
gegen die er heftig Einspruch erhebt, nicht nur, um
sich von den traditionell mit Dichtung verbunde-
nen niederen Dämonen zu distanzieren, sondern um
seinen Monismus der Inspiration zu behaupten, das
heißt das göttliche Monopol darauf, als Quelle legi-
timer Enthusiasmen zu wirken. Poetische Praxis, das

short poetic suras, stands at the beginning of textual production. Poetic recitation is, indeed, the fertile soil for the emergence of new texts; at the same time, its source of inspiration is the one God. This is shown in Q 73, which alludes to a vigil:

You, enfolded in your cloak!
Stay up throughout the night, all but a small part of it, half,
or a little less, or a little more;
recite slowly and distinctly:
We shall send a momentous message down to you [...]
so celebrate the name of your Lord
and devote yourself wholeheartedly to Him!
He is Lord of the east and west, there is no god but Him,
so take Him as your Protector!

The nucleus of the Quran thus emerges, according to its own testimony, from the living practice of the now Arabicized Psalm recitation.[57] Diverse connections to the Psalms, not only as texts, but also as scenarios of a divine-human conversation, bear witness to the development of the earliest Quran from a psalmistic – purely oral, not yet scriptural – piety. Remaining in their Arab tradition of art and yet also standing in the typological succession of the biblically educated devout, the community of listeners gradually attained to a new self-image: they saw themselves as spiritual descendants of the Israelites, whose leader, Moses, in Egypt, like they themselves

heißt unter den frühesten Hörern: psalmodierende Rezitation jener poetischen Kurzsuren, die am Anfang der Textproduktion stehen – Poesie-Rezitation ist zwar der Nährboden für die Entstehung neuer Texte, aber ihre Inspirationsquelle ist der *eine* Gott, wie Q 73 zeigt, wo auf eine Vigil angespielt ist:

Du Eingehüllter,
steh des Nachts, den größten Teil,
die Hälfte, oder zieh davon etwas ab,
oder füge etwas hinzu
und trag die Lesung vor in deutlichem Vortrag.
Dann werden wir dir gewichtige Rede aufgeben [...]
So gedenke des Namens deines Herrn und gib dich ihm ganz hin!
Er ist der Herr des Sonnenaufgangs und Niedergangs.
Kein Gott außer ihm! Nimm ihn zum Schutzherrn!

Der Nucleus des Koran entsteht also seinem eigenen Zeugnis nach aus der lebendigen Praxis der nun arabisierten Psalmenrezitation.[57] Unübersehbare Verbindungen zu den Psalmen nicht nur als Texten, sondern auch als Szenarien eines gott-menschlichen Gesprächs, bezeugen die Entwicklung des frühesten Koran aus einer psalmistischen – rein mündlichen, noch nicht Schrift-bezogenen – Frömmigkeit. In ihrer arabischen Kunsttradition verbleibend und zugleich in der typologischen Nachfolge biblisch gebildeter Frommer stehend gelangt die Hörergemeinde allmählich zu einem neuen Selbstbild: Sie verstehen sich als spirituelle Nachfahren der Israeliten, deren

in Mecca, were hard-pressed by a society that denied faith in the one God.

Two congenial prophets: Moses and Muhammad

This state of affairs is the basis for understanding the formative part of the Quran, the so-called middle Meccan suras. It is conceded more and more in recent research regarding these texts that the Quran interprets extant traditional knowledge in a new, typological way. Moses and the »type« of the prophet as such, becomes a model for Muhammad. Yet the process of appropriation of biblical knowledge is from the outset not linearly one-sided. It also operates regressively: The community of listeners – almost always ignored in research – transformed the older traditions by impressing on them the stamp of their own Arab late-antique reality. This also happens with Moses who is closely connected to the holy place of the Israelites, Jerusalem, in the Quran. It is worth casting a passing glance on the idea of Jerusalem here. It accompanies the entire Quranic development, but not without going through substantial changes. Jerusalem not only stands for the empirically known place, but rather for the monotheistic

Führer, Mose in Ägypten wie sie selbst in Mekka von einer den Eingottglauben verweigernden Gesellschaft bedrängt wurde.

Zwei kongeniale Propheten: Mose und Muhammad

Dieser Stand der Dinge ist die Grundlage für das Verständnis des formativen Teils des Koran, der sogenannten mittelmekkanischen Suren. Für diesen Textbestand wird in der neueren Forschung immer öfter konzediert, dass der Koran vorfindliches Traditionswissen typologisch neu liest. Mose, überhaupt der Typus des Propheten, wird zum Modell für Muhammad. Doch ist der Prozess der Aneignung biblischen Wissens von Anfang an nicht linear-einseitig, sondern wirkt sich auch rückläufig aus: Die – in der Forschung fast immer ausgeblendete – Hörergemeinde transformiert die älteren Traditionen, indem sie ihnen den Stempel ihrer eigenen arabischen spätantiken Realität aufdrückt. Das geschieht auch mit Mose, der im Koran eng mit dem Heiligtum der Israeliten, mit Jerusalem, verbunden ist. Im Folgenden sei deswegen ein Seitenblick auf die Jerusalem-Idee geworfen. Sie begleitet die gesamte koranische Entwicklung, nicht ohne substantielle Wandlungen zu erfahren. Jerusalem steht dabei nicht nur für den empirisch bekannten Ort, sondern für das

sanctuary as such, an emblem for the biblical tradition warranted by scripture.

Jerusalem is the first direction of prayer, *qibla*, for the community of listeners – analogous to the contemporary Jews. Its introduction is not explicitly mentioned in the Quran. Various indications suggest, however, that it was introduced a few years after the beginning of the proclamation along with the other major liturgical innovation, the introduction of the community prayer, the *fātiḥa*. Indeed, the new community of listeners forming in Mecca no longer lives from the proclamation alone but also from their liturgy, from the enactment of the Quranic texts in a ritual of prayer. By replacing the local Kaaba with the biblical sanctuary in Jerusalem it transferred its sacred space from the real Mecca to a textual space constructed from traditions.[58] The space around Jerusalem is the area of the activities of the patriarchs and thus also the land of the Israelites who were once guided by Moses. The community – in a situation of internal exile in Mecca – turns to Jerusalem as its spiritual home, a step that is comparable to that of the earlier Babylonian Jews. It does not do this, however, without also bringing the holy place in Jerusalem typologically closer to their own Meccan holy place, the Kaaba. Indeed, in prayer they do not direct themselves to the biblical temple, the house of God, *bayt*, but – similar to the Meccan sanctuary – to a »place of prayer« occupied by humans, a *masdjid*. The Messen-

monotheistische Heiligtum schlechthin, als Emblem für die biblische, durch Schrift verbürgte Tradition.

Jerusalem ist die erste Gebetsrichtung (*qibla*) der Hörergemeinde – ganz analog zu den zeitgenössischen Juden. Ihre Einführung ist im Koran nicht explizit bezeugt, vieles spricht aber dafür, dass sie einige Jahre nach Beginn der Verkündigung zusammen mit der anderen großen liturgischen Neuerung, dem Gemeindegebet, der *Fātiḥa*, eingeführt wurde. Denn die neue, sich in Mekka herausbildende Hörer-Gemeinde lebt nicht mehr von der Verkündigung allein, sondern auch von ihrer Liturgie, von der Inszenierung der Korantexte in einem Gebetsritual. Indem die Gemeinde dieses Ritual nun nicht mehr mit der lokalen Kaaba assoziiert, sondern es auf das biblische Heiligtum Jerusalem hin ausrichtet, verlegt sie ihren sakralen Raum aus dem realen Mekka heraus in einen aus Traditionen konstruierten Textraum.[58] Der Umkreis Jerusalems ist der Handlungsraum der Erzväter – und damit auch das Land der Israeliten, die einst von Mose geführt wurden. Die Gemeinde, in Mekka in einer Situation des inneren Exils, wendet sich, vergleichbar den babylonischen Juden, nach Jerusalem als ihrer spirituellen Heimat. Sie tut das aber nicht, ohne das Jerusalemer Heiligtum typologisch dem eigenen mekkanischen, der Kaaba, anzunähern. Denn man richtet sich im Gebet nicht zum biblischen Tempel, dem Haus (*bayt*) Gottes, sondern – analog zum mekkanischen Hei-

ger himself was transferred to this *masdjid* in a dream vision at night, to which Q 17:1 alludes:

Glory to Him who made His servant travel by night
[*asrā bi-ʿabdihi*]
from the sacred place of worship [i. e. the Kaaba]
to the furthest place of worship,
whose surroundings We have blessed,
[i.e. those in the Holy Land]
to show him some of our signs:
He alone is the All Hearing, the All Seeing.

The identification of the destination of the »night journey« with the Jerusalem sanctuary – which belongs to the Israelites (reclaimed as spiritual ancestors) and is therefore also connected with Moses – suggests the interpretation of the visionary translocation in the sense of an *Imitatio Mosis* on the part of Muhammad. Moses was also brought up to an elevated place to receive the tablets. Even more closely related to Moses is the movement itself. The nocturnal displacement of the Messenger to the holy place of the Israelites is modeled after the Exodus. Moses's commission to lead the Israelites out of Egypt is phrased quite similarly in the Quran. Moses' commission, »Go forth with my servants«, *asri bi-ʿibādī*, can be clearly heard resounding in *asrā bi-ʿabdihi*. As with Moses so also with Muhammad: the narrative is concerned with an experience of liberation. With Muhammad, how-

ligtum – zu einer von Menschen besetzten »Gebetsstätte«, einem *masdjid.* Zu diesem *masdjid* ist der Verkünder selbst in einer nächtlichen Traumvision entrückt worden, worauf Q 17:1 anspielt:

Gepriesen sei, der seinen Diener nachts ausziehen ließ
(asra bi-'abdihi)
von der heiligen Gebetsstätte [der Kaaba]
zu der ferneren Gebetsstätte,
die wir ringsum gesegnet haben
[die im Heiligen Land gelegen ist],
um ihm von unseren Zeichen zu zeigen.
Er ist der Hörende, der Sehende.

Die Identifizierung der Zielorts der »Nachtreise« mit
dem Jerusalemer Heiligtum, das den – als spirituelle Vorfahren reklamierten – Israeliten gehört und
damit auch mit Mose verbunden ist, legt die Deutung der Traumentrückung im Sinne einer Imitatio Mosis seitens Muhammads nahe. Auch Mose war
zum Erhalt der Tafeln auf einen Gottesberg entrückt
worden. Noch deutlicher auf Mose bezogen ist aber
die Bewegung selbst: Die nächtliche Versetzung des
Verkünders hin zu dem Heiligtum der Israeliten ist
dem Exodus nachgebildet: Moses Auftrag, die Israeliten aus Ägypten zu führen, ist im Koran ganz ähn-
lich phrasiert; das an Mose gerichtete »Zieh aus mit
meinen Dienern« *(asri bi-'ibādī)* klingt hier mit *asrā*
bi-'abdihi noch deutlich durch. Es geht wie bei Mose
auch bei Muhammad um eine Befreiung, nun aber
um die Befreiung des Gesandten selbst. Er wird be-

ever, it is a liberation of the Messenger himself. He is freed from the oppression of the overpowering opponents in Mecca whose holy place nevertheless remains unquestioned as a point of departure and as a model for the »distant holy place.« The »Exodus of the Prophet« is reduced from the broad framework of the collective experience of a people of faith to an individual experience, but it also leads into the »blessed« land, the Promised Land.

Those listeners who did not recognize the Moses typology took offence at the empirical improbability of the event. The displacement in the dream, which was only hinted at, drew strong criticism from the pagan contemporaries, as is reported in the sīra. They did not measure the reported experience in terms of the precedent of Moses, but in categories of geographical distance. Īliyā, that is, Aelia Capitolina, as Jerusalem was called at that time, is far too far away to be reached from Mecca in a single night. This allegation, which we know from the Islamic tradition, is not reflected in the Quran. By contrast, in the same sura 17 (17:93) the opponents come with an even bolder challenge to the Prophet. He should go on a journey to heaven, a displacement not to the earthly, but to the heavenly Jerusalem. The Messenger counters this by disclaiming any supernatural power for himself:

freit aus der Bedrängnis durch übermächtige Gegner in Mekka, dessen Heiligtum aber dennoch als Ausgangsort und als Modell für das »fernere Heiligtum« unangetastet bleibt. Der »Exodus des Propheten« ist zwar aus dem breiten Rahmen der kollektiven Erfahrung eines Glaubensvolkes zu einer individuellen Erfahrung verkleinert, doch führt auch er in das »gesegnete«, das Gelobte Land.

Hörer, die diese Mose-Typologie nicht erkannten, nahmen an der empirischen Unwahrscheinlichkeit des Ereignisses Anstoß. Die nur in Andeutung berichtete Traumversetzung löste, wie die Sīra berichtet, heftige Kritik der paganen Zeitgenossen aus, die die berichtete Erfahrung nicht an der Mose-Präzedenz, sondern in den Kategorien geographischer Entfernung maßen. Īliyā, also Aelia Capitolina, wie Jerusalem im zeitgenössischen Gebrauch hieß, sei viel zu weit entfernt, um von Mekka aus in einer einzigen Nacht erreicht zu werden. Dieser uns aus der islamischen Überlieferung bekannte Vorwurf wird im Koran nicht reflektiert. Dagegen treten die Gegner noch in derselben Sure 17 (17:93) mit einer noch kühneren Herausforderung an den Propheten heran: Er soll eine Himmelsreise antreten, eine Ortsversetzung nicht in das irdische, sondern in das himmlische Jerusalem. Ihr tritt der Verkünder entgegen, indem er jede übernatürliche Kraft von sich weist:

They say, We will not believe for you until you [...] ascend into the heavens – even then, we will not believe in your ascension until you send a real book down for us to read. Say, Glory be to my Lord! Am I anything but a mortal, a messenger?

The opponents interpret the words of the Prophet in the literal sense. He who often claimed to owe his speech to a heavenly scripture (like Moses who received the heavenly scripture in the form of tablets), is now challenged to display the transcendent scripture materially. In the religious milieu of the Quran, revelations had long taken on written form. The image of scrolls and illuminated codices of the Jews and Christians may have been in the mind of the challengers. The Quranic message, which was mediated in an exclusively oral way, apparently lacked authorization. That which actually makes the pagans unbelievers, however, is not their maximal demands. It is their fundamental refusal to translate the allegedly everyday speech into typological speech, which relies on scripture as its reference, not as its physical medium. The assertion of the Quranic claim to validity as a new manifestation of the universal transcendent scripture stands and falls with the acceptance of typology as hermeneutics.

Precisely because typology was finally proven to be the successful model, because the typologi-

Sie sprechen: Wir werden dir nicht glauben, bis du selbst [...] in den Himmel aufsteigst. Und deinen Aufstieg werden wir nicht glauben, bis du eine Schrift zu uns herabbringst, die wir lesen können. Sprich: Preis sei Gott! Bin ich denn etwas anderes als ein menschlicher Gesandter?

Die Gegner deuten die Worte des Propheten im Literalsinn. Er, der oft beansprucht hatte, seine Rede einer himmlischen Schrift zu verdanken, Mose vergleichbar, der die himmlische Schrift in Gestalt der Tafeln erhielt, wird nun herausgefordert, die transzendente Schrift auch materialiter vorzuweisen. Offenbarungen haben im religiösen Milieu des Koran längst schriftliche Form angenommen, den Herausforderern dürfte das Bild von Schriftrollen und Prachtkodizes der Juden und Christen vorschweben. Der ausschließlich mündlich vermittelten koranischen Botschaft mangelte es offenbar an Autorisierung. Was die Paganen aber eigentlich zu Ungläubigen macht, sind nicht ihre Maximalforderungen, es ist ihre grundsätzliche Verweigerung der Übersetzung von vermeintlicher Alltagsrede in typologische Rede, die sich auf Schrift als ihre Referenz, nicht als ihr physisches Medium, beruft. Die Durchsetzung des koranischen Geltungsanspruchs als eine neue Manifestation der universalen transzendenten Schrift steht und fällt mit der Durchsetzung der Typologie als Hermeneutik.

Gerade weil sich aber Typologie letztendlich als das Erfolgsmodell erweisen sollte, weil der typolo-

cally speaking Quran became a holy scripture, the long path towards its acceptance, that is, the controversial status of typological speech throughout the proclamation, has remained virtually unnoticed in research. If one reads the Quran synchronically, as is generally practiced, as a *fait accompli*, this counter-movement on the part of outsider pagans – who challenge the new believers to translate the world of the biblical text into their actual Arab reality – does not come into view. To what extent are the biblical figures also relevant for Mecca? This is their question. Evidence of such interweaving of the biblical and the Arabic cannot be demonstrated through the »simple typology,« as addressed above (that is, positing of biblical and historical persons and events, especially Moses and Muhammad, the Exodus and the visionary translocation, on the same level). The required typology here is the stronger figure of »promise and fulfillment«. It connects with Abraham, who, as patriarch, stands deeply in the biblical tradition, yet, genealogically, as the progenitor of the Arabs, also displays Arabic traits.

gisch sprechende Koran zu einer heiligen Schrift auf-
rückte, ist der lange Weg hin zu ihrer Akzeptanz, das
heißt der (zeit der Verkündigung) kontroverse Status typologischer Rede in der Forschung so gut wie
unbeachtet geblieben. Wenn man, wie es gegenwärtig fast generell Usus ist, den Koran synchron, als *fait
accompli*, liest, tritt jene Gegenbewegung seitens der
außenstehenden Paganen nicht in den Blick, die die
neuen Gläubigen zu einer Übersetzung der biblischen
Textwelt in ihre reale arabische Wirklichkeit heraus-
fordern. Inwiefern sind – so ihre Frage – die biblischen Figuren auch für Mekka relevant? Der Nach-
weis einer solchen Verflechtung von Biblischem und
Arabischem ist durch die eben vorgestellte »einfache
Typologie«, das heißt die Auf-Augenhöhe-Platzie-
rung von biblischen und zeitgeschichtlichen Personen und Ereignissen – vor allem Moses und Muhammads, des Exodus und der Traumentrückung – allein
nicht zu leisten. Die hier geforderte Typologie ist die
stärkere Figur der »Erfüllung einer Verheißung«. Sie
verbindet sich mit Abraham, der als Erzvater tief in
der biblischen Tradition steht, der aber genealogisch
als Stammvater der Araber auch arabische Züge trägt.

The Meccan Quran and Abraham's sacrifice:
Biblicization of the Arab worldview

Now we shall take a look at the configuration of late-antique Abrahamic traditions in the Quran, understood as the proclamation which the Prophet Muhammad recited to a growing community of listeners in the 7th century. By this time, in Judaism prophecy was considered to have long ceased. It was replaced with »interpretation« since religious speech was – as one saw it – already available in a binding and authoritative textual form. There was a recognized collection of biblical writings that was, essentially, only to be commented on. The new type of religious speaker was therefore, in the post-biblical horizon, no longer the prophet but the wise man, the *hakham*.[59] In Muhammad, one certainly should see both, a late Arab prophet[60] and a contemporary interpreter of the biblical traditions, a *hakham*. Among his listeners (about whom there are no reports outside of the Quran) we can imagine – for the time he was active in Mecca – Arabic native-speakers educated in late antique lore. These should have been for the most part syncretists who were already familiar with the most important Jewish and Christian traditions. In the course of the proclamation, more and more people who considered of theological matters were gathering around this group.

Der mekkanische Koran und das Abrahamsopfer: Biblisierung des arabischen Weltbilds

Werfen wir nun einen Blick auf die Konfiguration spätantiker Abraham-Traditionen im Koran, verstanden als die Verkündigung, die der Prophet Muḥammad im 7. Jahrhundert einer wachsenden Gemeinde von Hörern vortrug. Prophetie galt im jüdischen Umkreis um diese Zeit längst erloschen. Sie war ersetzt durch »Auslegung«, denn religiöse Rede lag – wie man es sah – bereits in verbindlicher Form verschriftlicht vor, es gab eine anerkannte Sammlung biblischer Schriften, die es im Wesentlichen nur noch zu kommentieren galt. Der neue Typus des religiösen Sprechers war daher im biblischen Horizont nicht mehr der Prophet, sondern der Weise, der *hakham*.[59] Man hat in Muḥammad gewiss beides, einen spät gekommenen arabischen Propheten[60] und einen aktuellen Ausleger der biblischen Traditionen, einen *hakham*, zu sehen. Unter seinen Hörern, über die wir außerhalb des Koran keine Nachrichten besitzen, haben wir uns für seine mekkanische Wirkungszeit arabischsprachige spätantike Gebildete vorzustellen, am ehesten Synkretisten, die mit den wichtigsten jüdischen und christlichen Traditionen bereits vertraut sind und um die sich im Verlauf der Verkündigung immer mehr theologisch Interessierte gruppieren.

It must have been a concern to this emerging community to »update« the biblical message, to make it relevant for their special situation as a monotheistic renewal movement within a society that was pagan or syncretistically dominated.[61] With this, they followed the hermeneutics of the older traditions which had long read the biblical texts typologically. In their exegesis, Abraham had acquired a special status as the paradigmatically righteous one. It is therefore astonishing to see that the Quranic Abraham does not initially figure prominently among the rest of the prophets. After his name had been associated with the authority of divine scriptures at a very early stage (Q 87:19) and had also been connected with the virtue of exemplary fidelity (Q 53:37), Abraham becomes – still in the early Meccan phase – the protagonist of one of the first Quranic stories ever. In his old age, the birth of a son is announced to him (Q 51:24–37; cf. Gen 18:1–20) – an event that is, as Nicolai Sinai argues convincingly, to be interpreted typologically within the Quran: a righteous man who is a stranger in his own society, as is also the case with Muhammad, can count on divine assistance.

Dieser sich herausbildenden Gemeinde musste daran gelegen sein, die biblische Botschaft zu »aktualisieren«, sie für ihre besondere Situation als monotheistische Erneuerungsbewegung inmitten einer pagan bzw. synkretistisch beherrschten Gesellschaft relevant zu machen.[61] Man folgte dabei der Hermeneutik der beiden älteren Traditionen, die biblische Texte längst typologisch lasen. In ihrer Exegese war Abraham ein besonderer Status als Gerechter schlechthin zugewachsen. Es ist daher erstaunlich, dass der koranische Abraham zunächst vor den übrigen Propheten nicht prominent hervorragt. Nachdem sein Name sehr früh einmal mit der Autorität göttlicher Schriften (Q 87:19) assoziiert und ein weiteres Mal mit der Tugend exemplarischer Treue verbunden worden war (Q 53:37), wird Abraham – immer noch frühmekkanisch – Protagonist einer der ersten koranischen Erzählungen überhaupt. Ihm wird (Q 51:24–37, vergleiche Genesis 18,1–20) im hohen Alter die Geburt eines Sohnes angekündigt – ein Ereignis, das (wie Nicolai Sinai überzeugend argumentiert) innerkoranisch typologisch zu deuten ist: Ein in seiner Gesellschaft fremder Gerechter – wie es Muḥammad auch ist – kann auf göttlichen Beistand bauen.

Sura 51:24–37 reads:

24   *Have you heard the story of the honoured guests of Abraham?*
25   *They went in to see him and said, ›Peace.‹ ›Peace‹, he said,*
       [adding to himself] ›These people are strangers.‹
26   *He turned quickly to his household, brought out a fat calf,*
27   *and placed it before them. ›Will you not eat?‹ he said,*
28   *beginning to be afraid of them, but they said, ›Do not be*
       afraid.‹ They gave him good news of a son ·
       who would be gifted with knowledge.
29   *His wife then entered with a loud cry, struck her face and*
       said, ›A barren old woman?‹
30   *But they said, ›It will be so. This is what your Lord said, and*
       He is the Wise, the All Knowing.‹
31   *Abraham said, ›What is your errand, messengers?‹*
32   *They said, ›We are sent to a people lost in sin,*
33   *to bring down rocks of clay,*
34   *marked by your Lord for those who exceed all bounds.‹*
35   *We brought out such believers as were there –*
36   *We found only one household devoted to God –*
37   *and left the town to be a sign for those*
       who fear the painful punishment.

There follows several »stories of retribution«:

38   *There is another sign in Moses: We sent him to Pharaoh with*
       clear authority.
39   *Pharaoh turned away with his supporters, saying,*
       ›This is a sorcerer, or maybe a madman‹,
40   *so We seized him and his forces*
       and threw them into the sea: he was to blame.

Sure 51:24–37 lautet:

24 *Kam zu dir die Kunde von Abrahams Gästen, den geehrten?*
25 *Als sie bei ihm eintraten und sprachen: Friede.*
    Er sprach: Friede. Unbekannte Leute.
26 *Da ging er hinein zu den Seinen und brachte ein fettes Kalb*
    herbei,
27 *und setzte es ihnen vor: Wollt ihr denn nicht essen?*
28 *Und es überkam ihn Furcht vor ihnen.*
    Sie sprachen: Fürchte dich nicht!
    Und sie verkündeten ihm einen klugen Knaben.
29 *Da kam seine Frau herbei,*
    sie schlug sich auf die Wangen und rief:
    Eine unfruchtbare Alte!
30 *Sie sprachen: So spricht dein Herr.*
    Er ist der Wissende und Weise.
31 *Abraham sprach: Was habt ihr vor, Gesandte?*
32 *Sie sprachen: Wir sind zu einem Volk gesandt, das sündigt,*
33 *Steine aus Lehm über sie zu schicken,*
34 *bei deinem Herrn für diejenigen gebrannt,*
    die nicht Maß halten.
35 *Doch führten wir die, die in der Stadt gläubig waren, hinaus.*
36 *Es gab in ihr nur ein einziges Haus von Gottergebenen.*
37 *In ihr sind Zeichen für die,*
    die die schmerzliche Strafe fürchten.

Es folgen mehrere »Straflegenden«:

38 *Und in Mose,*
    als wir ihn mit klarer Vollmacht zu Pharao sandten.
39 *Der wandte sich zu seinem Helfer und sprach:*
    Ein Zauberer oder Besessener!
40 *Da kamen wir über ihn und seine Truppen*
    und warfen sie ins Meer.
    Er verdiente sich die Strafe.

41   *There is another sign in the 'Ād:*
      We sent the life-destroying wind against them
42   *and it reduced everything it came up against to shreds.*
43   *And also in the Thamūd: it was said to them, ›Make the most*
      of your lives for a while‹,
44   *but they rebelled against their Lord's command,*
      so the blast took them. They looked on helplessly:
45   *they could not even remain standing,*
      let alone defend themselves.
46   *Before that We destroyed the people of Noah.*
      They were a truly sinful people!

The narrative about the promise to Abraham (v. 24–30) is important beyond its typology. It stands out clearly from the following sequence of stories which are all »legends of retribution« (Lot, Pharaoh, the 'Ād, Thamūd and the people of Noah), that is, stories that revolve around the punitive destruction of a rebellious people and the salvation of their divine messenger. Indeed, with the Abraham story, for the first time, the development of historical consciousness emerges. While the other stories do create an overarching temporal context, they nevertheless form a discontinuous history of ancient peoples who do not stand in genealogical succession with one another nor interact with one another. They primarily reflect the situation of the Prophet and, at the same time, provide an aetiological explanation of the ubiquituos presence of ruins in the local milieu, a problem that occupied ancient Arab society.[62] As in the biblical tradition where the future of Abraham's de-

41 *Und so auch in den ʿĀd.*
    Als wir den alles vernichtenden Wind über sie sandten,
42 *der nichts verschonte, und alles gleichsam morsch machte.*
43 *Und in den Thamūd. Als zu ihnen gesagt wurde:*
    Genießet eine Zeitlang! Eure Frist ist bemessen.
44 *Doch sie missachteten den Auftrag ihres Herrn.*
    Da überkam sie sehenden Auges der Donnerschlag.
45 *Sie konnten nicht standhalten und fanden keine Hilfe.*
46 *Und die Leute Noahs schon früher.*
    Sie waren frevlerische Leute.

Diese Verheißungsgeschichte (V. 24–30) ist aber auch über ihre Typologie hinaus von Bedeutung. Sie hebt sich deutlich von der ihr folgenden Sequenz von Erzählungen ab, die sämtlich – um Lot, Pharao, die ʿĀd, die Thamūd und die Leute Noahs kreisend – »Straflegenden« sind, das heißt Erzählungen, die um die strafweise Vernichtung eines unbotmäßigen Volkes und die Errettung ihres Gottesboten kreisen. Denn mit der Abraham-Geschichte bahnt sich erstmals die Entwicklung eines Geschichtsbewusstseins an: Während die weiteren Erzählungen zwar einen zeitübergreifenden Zusammenhang herstellen, bilden sie doch eine diskontinuierliche Geschichte der alten Völkerschaften ab, die untereinander in keiner genealogischen Sukzession stehen, noch auch in eine Interaktion eintreten. Sie spiegeln vornehmlich die Situation des Propheten und liefern zugleich eine ätiologische Erklärung für das die altarabische Gesellschaft beschäftigende Problem der Ubiquität von

scendants, the people of Israel, is made known to him (Gen 15:12–16), so also in the Quran, history begins with Abraham. He alone receives a promise with the announcement of an heir.

The story of the annunciation is retold repeatedly until it acquires something of a retrospective justification through, as Nicolai Sinai calls it, the »pericope of conflict«, the story of Abraham's battle against idolatry in his homeland. After Abraham has paid the high price for his commitment to monotheistic faith in the loss of his embeddedness in his clan and society, he receives the gift of the birth of a child in his old age.

The »pericope of conflict« is known not from the Bible but from Jewish literature alone. This narrative about the destruction of the idols, which is told eight times,[63] is initially far more influential for the Quranic image of Abraham than the story of the sacrifice. It presents Abraham as that biblical figure who intended to bring about the breakthrough of the sole worship of God in a pagan environment, like the Prophet Muhammad himself. Abraham successfully launched a social paradigm shift: the shift from a genealogical bond of the individual with clan and family to a *transcendent bond*, a relationship with God.[64] It is this transition that Muhammad's community in

Ruinenstätten in ihrer Lebenswelt.[62] Wie in der biblischen Tradition, der gemäß Abraham die Zukunft seiner Nachkommen, des Volkes Israel, eröffnet wird (Genesis 15,12–16), so beginnt auch im Koran erst mit Abraham Geschichte – ihm allein wird mit der Ankündigung eines Nachkommen eine Verheißung zuteil.

Die Ankündigungsgeschichte wird mehrfach wiedererzählt, bevor sie durch die von Nicolai Sinai sogenannte »Streitperikope«, die Erzählung von Abrahams Bekämpfung des Götzendienstes in seiner Heimat, gewissermaßen eine nachträgliche Rechtfertigung findet: Nachdem Abraham seinen Einsatz für den Eingottglauben teuer – mit dem Verlust der Aufgehobenheit in seinem Clan und seiner Gesellschaft – bezahlt hat, wird ihm zum Lohn noch im hohen Alter ein Nachkomme geschenkt.

Die Streitperikope ist nicht aus der Bibel, sondern erst aus der jüdischen Tradition bekannt. Diese Erzählung von der Zerstörung der Götzen, die acht Mal erzählt wird,[63] ist für das koranische Abrahambild zunächst noch weit prägender als das Opfer. Sie fokussiert Abraham als diejenige biblische Figur, die – wie der Prophet Muḥammad selbst – der Alleinverehrung Gottes in einer paganen Umwelt zum Durchbruch verhelfen will. Abraham hat erfolgreich einen sozialen Paradigmenwechsel eingeleitet: Den Wechsel von einer *genealogischen Bindung* des Einzelnen an Clan und Familie hin zu einer *transzendenten Bindung*, einer Bindung an Gott.[64] Es ist dieser Über-

Mecca had to bring about as well. Indeed, the anta-
gonism between pagans and monotheists in the po-
larized urban society demanded of each individual a
decision between loyalty to family or the new religion.

At this time the Quranic community was already
aware of their election as a »new people of God« according to the model of the Israelites. With their
turning from the pagan cult at the Kaaba and with
the orienting of their prayers to the Jerusalem sanctuary, they had entered a kind of »inner emigration.«
The orientation towards spiritual ancestors, the biblical figures, especially the patriarchs, took the place
of the orientation towards their genealogical ancestors.[65] What we witness here is the foundation
of a counter-history, a substitution of local history
founded on tribal solidarity with a spiritually-based
history following the tradition of the Israelites, the
Banū Isrā'īl. What is unheard of in tribal society –
the breaking away of an individual from his family
– is now a part of everyday life for many of Muhammad's listeners. It is Abraham who lends himself here
as an example, as a *typos* for a group of devout believers of a new kind. Abraham renounces his father because he did not cease in his idolatry. The story forms
the first part of the two-part story of Abraham in
sura 37. In Q 37:83–98 we read:

gang, den die Gemeinde Muḥammads in Mekka ihrerseits zu vollziehen hatte, denn die Gegnerschaft zwischen Paganen und Monotheisten innerhalb der polarisierten Stadtgesellschaft forderte von jedem Einzelnen eine Entscheidung zwischen Herkunft und neuer Religion.

Die koranische Gemeinde ist sich zu dieser Zeit bereits ihrer Erwählung als »neues Gottesvolk« nach dem Modell der Israeliten bewusst, sie hat sich mit der Abwendung vom paganen Kult an der Kaaba und ihrer Hinwendung zum Jerusalemer Heiligtum in eine Art »innere Emigration« begeben, in der an die Stelle der Orientierung an genealogischen Vorfahren eine Orientierung an spirituellen Vorfahren, den biblischen Personen, vor allem den Erzvätern, getreten ist.[65] Es ist die Grundlegung einer *counter-history*, einer Ersetzung der lokal auf tribale Solidarität gegründeten Geschichte durch eine spirituell basierte Geschichte, die an die Tradition der Israeliten, der *Banū Isrāʾīl* anschließt. Was in einer Stammesgesellschaft unerhört ist – die Lossagung eines Individuums von seiner Familie – gehört nun für viele Hörer Muḥammads zum Alltag. Es ist Abraham, der sich hier als Vorbild, als Typus einer Gruppe von Frommen neuen Schlages, anbietet. Abraham sagt sich von seinem Vater los, weil dieser nicht von seinem Götzendienst ablässt. Die Geschichte bildet den ersten Teil der zweiteiligen Abrahamerzählung in Sure 37. In Q 37:83–98 heißt es:

83   *Abraham belonged to the same group [as Noah]:*
84   *he came to his Lord with a devoted heart.*
85   *He said to his father and his people, ›What are you*
      worshipping?‹
86   *How can you choose false gods instead of the true God?*
87   *So what is your opinion about the Lord of the*
      Worlds?' […]
91   *He turned to their gods and said,*
92   *›Do you not eat? Why do you not speak?‹*
93   *Then he turned and struck them with his right arm.*
94   *His people hurried towards him,*
95   *but he said, ›How can you worship things*
      you carve with your own hands,
96   *when it is God who has created you*
      and all your handiwork?‹ […]
98   *They wanted to harm him, but We humiliated them.*

The sacrifice narrative
before and after its expansion

While in this narrative Abraham exchanged his bond
with his father for a bond with God (and thus traded
his genealogical pact for a divine covenant), in the
sacrifice narrative, the *Akedah*, it is the bond with his
son that he was ready to give up for his faithfulness
to God. The sacrifice story, which is told only once,
connects directly in Q 37:99–109, whereas the annunciation of the son (v. 101), which is taken up from
Q 52, recalls the important promise (*tabshīr*) prehis-
tory.

83 *Zu seiner (Noahs) Gemeinschaft gehört auch Abraham,*
84 *als er zu seinem Herrn mit lauterem Herzen kam,*
85 *als er zu seinem Vater und seinen Leuten sprach: Was betet ihr da an?*
86 *Strebt ihr aus Lüge Götter an – außer dem einen Gott?*
87 *Was denkt ihr denn vom Herrn der Welten? [...]*
91 *Dann wandte er sich den Götzen zu und sprach: Wollt ihr denn nicht essen?*
92 *Wie kommt es, dass ihr nicht sprecht?*
93 *Und er holte aus mit einem Schlag der Rechten gegen sie.*
94 *Da stürmten seine Leute auf ihn los.*
95 *Er sprach: Betet ihr etwa euer eigenes Schnitzwerk an?*
96 *Wo doch Gott euch erschaffen und euch Wissen gegeben hat?* [...]
98 *Sie planten gegen ihn eine List, wir aber machten sie zu den Unterlegenen.*

Die Opfer-Erzählung vor und nach ihrer Erweiterung

Während Abraham in dieser Geschichte seine Bindung zu seinem Vater für eine Bindung zu Gott eintauscht, seinen genealogischen Pakt also mit einem Gottesbund vertauscht, ist es in der Opfergeschichte, der Akedah, die Bindung zu seinem Sohn, die er bereit ist, für seine Treue zu Gott aufzugeben. Die Opfergeschichte, die nur ein einziges Mal erzählt wird, schließt direkt an in Q 37:99–109, wobei die aus Q 52 wiederaufgenommene Sohnesankündigung V. 101 die wichtige Verheißungs-(*tabshīr*)-Vorgeschichte wieder präsent macht:

99   *He said, ›I will go to my Lord: He is sure to guide me.*
100   *Lord, grant me a righteous son,‹*
101   *so We gave him the good news that he would have a patient son.*

102   *When he (Abraham) was about to perform the »run«
      with him (the son), Abraham said, ›My son, I have seen
      myself sacrificing you in a dream. What do you think?‹
      He said, ›Father, do as you are commanded and, God
      willing, you will find me steadfast.‹*

103   *When they had both submitted to God,
      and he had laid his son down on the side of his face,*
104   *We called out to him, ›Abraham,*
105   *you have fulfilled the dream.‹
      This is how We reward those who do good –*
106   *it was a test to prove [their true characters] –*
107   *We ransomed his son with a momentous sacrifice,*
108   *and We let him be praised by succeeding generations:*
109   *›Peace be upon Abraham!‹*[66]
110   *This is how We reward those who do good:*
111   *truly he was one of Our faithful servants.*

112   *We gave Abraham the good news of Isaac – a prophet
      and a righteous man –*
113   *and blessed him and Isaac too: some of their offspring
      were good, but some clearly wronged themselves.*

Without verse 102 (which was added later) and verse
112 f. (which were added even later) the story follows the pattern of the biblical account. Abraham
leaves his father and his society and, trusting in divine guidance, he emigrates. His prayer for a son is

99   *Er sprach: Ich gehe hin zu meinem Herrn, Er wird mich lei-*
       ten.

100 *Herr, schenk mir einen von den Frommen!*

101 *Da kündigten wir ihm einen sanften Knaben an.*

      102 *Als er mit ihm soweit gekommen war,*
            den Lauf zu vollziehen,
            sprach er: Mein Sohn, ich sah im Traum,
            dass ich dich opfern soll.
            So sieh, was du dazu meinst.
            Er sprach: Mein Vater, tu was dir befohlen wird,
            du wirst mich, so Gott will, geduldig finden.

103 *Als sich die beiden* [in Gottes Willen] *ergeben hatten,*
      und er ihn auf die Schläfe geworfen hatte,

104 *da riefen wir ihn an: Abraham,*

105 *du hast den Traum erfüllt.*
      So lohnen wir denen, die Gutes tun!

106 *Dies ist eine deutliche Prüfung.*

107 *Durch ein gewaltiges Schlachtopfer schafften wir Ersatz für*
      ihn,

108 *und wir ließen für die Späteren den Spruch zurück:*

109 *Segen sei über Abraham!*[66]

110 *So belohnen wir die, die Gutes tun.*

111 *Er war einer unserer gläubigen Diener.*

      112 *Und wir verkündigten ihm Isaak,*
            einen Propheten, einen der Gerechten.

      113 *Wir segneten ihn und Isaak,*
            unter ihren Nachkommen sind Gerechte und solche,
            die sich selbst ins Unrecht setzen.

Ohne den später hinzugefügten Vers 102 (und unter Nichtberücksichtigung der noch späteren Verse 112 f.) gelesen wird die Geschichte zunächst nach dem Muster des biblischen Berichts erzählt: Abraham verlässt seinen Vater und seine Gesellschaft und

heard (v. 101). With the order to sacrifice being apparently known, the story begins with the first step towards carrying it out (v. 103). As in the biblical text, the sacrifice is eventually thwarted by divine intervention. Yet Abraham had passed a great test (v. 106, see Gen 22:1). According to the biblical text (Gen 22:16 f.), his willingness to offer extreme devotion to God will be rewarded with the privileging of his descendants who shall henceforth be justified by the »merits of their fathers.« In the Quranic text, by contrast, Abraham is rewarded with a mere blessing conferring honor, a eulogy. In the new community his name is henceforth to be connected with the formula: »peace be upon him« *'alayhi l-salām*. This transformation of a prophecy into a liturgical convention, for the community keeps the figure of Abraham present among the devout universally. It does not yet, however, privilege him above others, for other prophets receive the same eulogy in Q 37. That this history will acquire, in the course of Muhammad's ministry in Medina, a crucial religious and political significance, is not yet evident from this core version.

The matter, however, did not stop with this version. The story was expanded later in Medina with important details (as is recognizable with the overly long prose-verse 102): first with an explicit declara-

wandert im Vertrauen auf göttliche Leitung aus. Sein Gebet um einen Sohn wird erhört (V. 101). Der Auftrag zum Opfer ist offenbar bekannt, die Geschichte setzt gleich ein mit dem ersten Schritt zu seiner Ausführung, V. 103. Wie im biblischen Text wird das Opfer aber durch göttliche Intervention schließlich vereitelt. Doch hat Abraham auch so bereits eine schwere Prüfung (Vers 106, vergleiche Genesis 22,1) bestanden. Dem biblischen Text (Genesis 22,16 f.) zufolge wird seine Bereitschaft zur äußersten Hingabe an Gott belohnt mit der Privilegierung seiner Nachkommen, die fortan durch die »Verdienste ihrer Väter« gerechtfertigt sein sollen. Im koranischen Text dagegen wird Abraham lediglich mit einem ehrenden Segensspruch, einer Eulogie, belohnt: Sein Name soll für die neue Gemeinde fortan mit der Formel: »Segen über ihm«, *'alayhi l-salām*, verbunden werden. Diese Verwandlung einer Prophezeiung in eine liturgische Konvention für die Gemeinde hält die Gestalt Abrahams bei den Frommen insgesamt präsent. Sie privilegiert ihn jedoch noch nicht vor anderen, denn in Q 37 erhalten auch weitere Propheten dieselbe Eulogie. – Dass die Geschichte im Zuge von Muḥammads Wirkungszeit in Medina eine zentrale religionspolitische Bedeutung erhalten wird, zeichnet sich in dieser Kernversion zunächst noch nicht ab.

Bei dieser Version blieb es jedoch nicht, die Geschichte wurde später, in Medina – erkennbar an dem überlangen Prosavers 102 – um wichtige Details erweitert, zunächst um eine ausdrückliche Zu-

tion of the son's consent to his own sacrifice. This provides legitimacy for Abraham's intention: The son was old enough – as one interpretation holds – to be able to decide for himself. According to the most likely interpretation, however, he was already involved in the *ḥajj* rites (which call for a »run« between two small holy places, Al-Ṣafā and Al-Marwah).[67] The »revision« of the Quranic reading – which puts the leading role of Abraham (with whom, according to verse 83, the story is supposed to be concerned) on the son (who remains without a name) – may have been made in Medina in engagement with the exegetical readings of the Jews there. Indeed, the rabbinic reading also included Isaac as an active player in the sacrifice. It also no longer allowed for the monstrosity of the sacrifice of Abraham's son without his authorization. In its place came a shared act of obedience of father *and* son.[68] Initially, in the core version, the story was concerned with Abraham's obedience, then, in the extended version, it becomes concerned with the patience and solidarity of the son. If one reads both stories in Q 37 together, the destroying of the idols, the »pericope of conflict,« which calls for the separation from the father, and the Akedah story which calls for the forfeiting of the son, then Abraham appears in a double sense as a representative of a clear position in the dispute between *genealogical* bond and *religious* relationship.

stimmungserklärung des Sohnes zu seiner eigenen
Opferung. Sie soll Abrahams Absicht legitimieren:
Der Sohn war alt genug, um – so eine Interpretation – selbst entscheiden zu können. Nach der wahr-
scheinlichsten Interpretation war er bereits an den
ḥadjdj-Riten (die einen »Lauf« zwischen zwei kleinen
Heiligtümern, al-Ṣafā und al-Marwah vorsehen) beteiligt.[67] Die »Revision« der koranischen Lesart, die
nun die Hauptrolle von Abraham, um den es ja laut
Ankündigung (V. 83) eigentlich gehen sollte, auf
den – namenlos bleibenden – Sohn verlegt, dürfte in
Medina in Auseinandersetzung mit den exegetischen
Lektüren der dortigen Juden vorgenommen worden
sein, denn auch die rabbinische Lektüre beteiligte
Isaak an dem Opfer, auch sie ließ die Monstrosität
eines eigenmächtigen Sohnesopfers durch Abraham
nicht mehr zu; an seine Stelle trat ein gemeinschaft-
licher Gehorsamsakt von Vater *und* Sohn.[68] Es geht
zunächst – in der Kernversion – um Abrahams Ge-
horsam, dann in der erweiterten Fassung um die Ge-
duld und Solidarität des Sohnes. Liest man beide Geschichten in Q 37 zusammen, die Götzenzertrüm-
merung, »Streitperikope«, die die Trennung vom
Vater fordert, und die Gehorsamsbereitschaft, die
den Verzicht auf den Sohn fordert, so erscheint Abraham in doppelter Weise als Vertreter einer eindeu-
tigen Position im Streit zwischen *genealogischer* und
religiöser Bindung.

Abraham and the Meccan form of worship

Is the image of Abraham, which is emerging here, reflected in the piety of the Meccan community? Let us look at the state of ritual in Mecca more closely. We may presume that the core element of cultic activities was the ritual prayer, which is often referred to in the Meccan suras. That its performative form – consisting of postures of humility with short formulaic accompanying texts – goes back to the early Quranic community is very likely since these gestures, the bowing, *rukū'*, the standing, *qiyām*, and the prostration, *sujūd*, were often called for by command in Mecca. Likewise, the text elements, which went before each sequence of prayer – short suras introduced by the *fātiḥa* – were probably current in the emerging community.[69] The prayer ritual in its Meccan form is an ascetic exercise – recitations as well as entire prayer sequences are called for particularly at nighttime (see Q 73) – which seems to be most closely related to monastic ascetic rites. Role models for the expected spiritual disposition seem to be devout Christians whose »crying« with the hearing of the recitation is counted as meritorious (see Q 17:109), while this emotional reaction of crying is missed in those irreverent hearers of the Prophet who use to laugh instead (see Q 84:22).

Abraham und der mekkanische Kultus

Schlägt sich das hier entstehende Abrahambild auch in der Frömmigkeit der mekkanischen Gemeinde nieder? Sehen wir uns den Stand des Ritus in Mekka dazu genauer an: Als das Herzstück der Frömmigkeit dürfen wir das Ritualgebet voraussetzen, auf das in den mekkanischen Suren oft rekurriert wird. Dass seine performative Gestalt – bestehend aus Demutshaltungen mit kurzen formularischen Begleittexten – schon auf die frühe koranische Gemeinde zurückgeht, ist sehr wahrscheinlich, da diese Gesten, das Sich-beugen (*rukūʿ*) das Stehen (*qiyām*) und das Sich-Niederwerfen (*sudjūd*) bereits in Mekka oft imperativisch anempfohlen werden. Ebenso sollten die jeder Gebetssequenz vorausgehenden Textelemente – kurze Suren, eingeführt von der *fātiḥa* – bereits für die sich herausbildende Gemeinde das Übliche gewesen sein.[69] In seiner mekkanischen Erscheinungsform ist der Gebetsritus eine asketische Übung – Rezitationen wie auch ganze Gebetssequenzen werden gerade für die Nachtzeit anempfohlen (siehe Q 73) –, die am nächsten monastischen asketischen Riten verwandt zu sein scheint. Vorbilder für die dazu erwartete Haltung scheinen christliche Fromme zu sein, denen ihr »Weinen« beim Hören der Rezitation als verdienstvoll angerechnet wird (siehe Q 17:109), während dieses Weinen bei den unehrerbietigen Hörern des Propheten selbst vermisst wird (siehe Q 84:22), die stattdessen lachen.

Initially, this ritual ceremony exhibits no direct connection to Abraham. Such a connection is nevertheless achieved during the Meccan development. As the sura structures of the middle Meccan period show – which are, at least through the Meccan period, meant to be liturgical speech – and as the worship service of the Quranic community as such shows, the recitation of the suras, even after the suras had become longer, is best understood as happening in the context of prayer, perhaps before the ritual part (because some suras end with an invitation to »praise,« that is, to the recitation of the *fātiḥa*). The sura texts most likely served as »librettos« for the verbal part of the worship services. If it is now to be held that the sura-structures of the middle Meccan period have a strong resemblance to the order of events in worship services in Judaism and in Christianity, inasmuch as a biblical reading (or a biblical story in the Quran) is, in each case, the central part, one may conclude that with this appreciation of the narratives at the climax of their respective suras, and thus the respective liturgical celebration, a new authority is attributed to the biblical figures as well.[70] The biblical horizon, which has now become important, manifests itself beyond this in the recitation of a congregational prayer, *al-fātiḥa*, which has the status of the Lord's Prayer in Christianity, and in the orienting of the direction of prayer to Jerusalem. Among the biblical characters that are now coming into the foreground, Abraham plays an increasingly important role as the recipient

Zunächst weist dieses Zeremoniell also keine direkte Verbindung zu Abraham auf, eine solche konstituiert sich jedoch im Verlauf der mekkanischen Entwicklung. Was die Surenstrukturen, die zumindest die mekkanische Zeit hindurch liturgische Rede sind, zeigen und was der Gottesdienst der koranischen Gemeinde als solcher nahelegt, ist, dass die Surenrezitation, auch nachdem die Suren länger geworden waren, am ehesten im Kontext von Gebeten erfolgte, vielleicht dem rituellen Teil vorangestellt, da einzelne Suren mit der Aufforderung zum »Lob«, das heißt zur Rezitation der *fātiḥa*, enden. Die Suren dürften als »Librettos« für den Wortgottesdienst gedient haben. Wenn nun festzustellen ist, dass die Surenstrukturen der mittelmekkanischen Zeit eine starke Ähnlichkeit zu den Gottesdienstabläufen in Judentum und Christentum aufweisen, insofern jeweils eine biblische Lesung (bzw. im Koran eine biblische Erzählung) im Mittelpunkt steht, so darf man daraus schließen, dass mit dieser Aufwertung der Erzählungen zur Klimax ihrer jeweiligen Sure und damit der jeweiligen gottesdienstlichen Feier auch den biblischen Figuren eine neue Autorität zukommt.[70] Der nun wichtig gewordene biblische Horizont manifestiert sich darüber hinaus in der Rezitation eines Gemeindegebets (*al-fātiḥa*), das den Rang des christlichen Vaterunsers behauptet, und der Einnahme der Gebetsrichtung nach Jerusalem. Unter den nun in den Vordergrund tretenden biblischen Figuren spielt Abraham als Empfänger einer Verheißung eine zu-

of a promise. The repeatedly narrated »pericope of *tabshīr*« and the »pericope of conflict« present him as bound in a special way to the transcendent sphere and as a valiant defender of the bond which is owed only to God, although his role still stands behind that of Moses. He also acquires a liturgical aura, in that after he passes the test he is distinguished with the eulogy *ʿalayhi l-salām*, »peace be upon him.« (though this does not privilege him above other prophets who receive a corresponding employ according to Q 37).

Abraham's significance expands, however, step by step. His family receives renewed attention with the long *Sūrat Yūsuf*, which was composed in an exceptionally artful style. Joseph is committed from his father Jacob to the values of his forefathers Abraham and Isaac (Q 12:6); before his fellow prisoners, he invokes the »faith of my fathers, Abraham, Isaac and Jacob« (Q 12:38) *millat ābāʾī*. This »faith of the fathers,« which includes the three patriarchs, points to the covenant of God with the patriarchs and is clearly still a part of the heritage of the *Banū Isrāʾīl*; it still does not attest an Abrahamic identity. This is initiated only when Abraham is, in the late-Meccan period, brought into connection with the sanctuary of the Kaaba; when he prays and implores the observance of the prayer ritual for himself and for some of his descendants, a *vaticinatio ex eventu*, Q 14:35–41:

nehmend wichtige Rolle. Die wiederholt erzählten *tabshīr-* und Streitperikopen präsentieren ihn als in besonderer Weise mit der transzendenten Sphäre verbunden und als streitbaren Verfechter der allein Gott geschuldeten Bindung, wenn auch seine Rolle noch hinter der des Mose zurücksteht. Auch erhält er eine liturgische Aura, indem er nach bestandener Prüfung mit der Eulogie »*ʿalayhi l-salām*« (»Segen sei auf ihm«) ausgezeichnet wird, wenn ihn dies auch noch nicht vor anderen Propheten privilegiert, die laut Q 37 eine entsprechende Eulogie erhalten.

Sukzessiv weitet sich seine Bedeutung jedoch aus. So erhält seine Sippe durch die lange und außergewöhnlich kunstvoll komponierte Sūrat Yūsuf erneute Aufmerksamkeit. Josef wird von seinem Vater Jakob auf die Werte seiner Vorfahren Abraham und Isaak verpflichtet (Q 12:6), er selbst beruft sich vor seinen Mitgefangenen auf die »Glaubensrichtung meiner Väter, Abraham, Isaak und Jakob« (Q 12:38) *millat ābā'ī*. Diese »Glaubensrichtung der Väter«, die die drei Erzväter einschließt, deutet auf den Gottesbund mit den Erzvätern und ist noch eindeutig Bestandteil des Erbes der *Banū Isrā'īl*, sie hat noch nichts mit einer abrahamitischen Identität zu tun. Diese bahnt sich erst an, als Abraham in Spätmekka mit dem Heiligtum der Kaaba in Verbindung gebracht wird und ein Gebet spricht, in dem er für sich und einige seiner Nachkommen die Einhaltung des Gebetsritus erfleht, eine *vaticinatio ex eventu*, Q 14:35–41:

35 *Remember when Abraham said, ›Lord, make this town safe!*
    Preserve me and my offspring from idolatry,
36 *Lord, the [idols] have led many people astray!*
    Anyone who follows me is with me,
    but as for anyone who disobeys me — You are surely forgiving
    and merciful.
37 *Our Lord, I have established some of my offspring*
    in an uncultivated valley, close to Your Sacred House,
    Lord, so that they may keep up the prayer.
    Make people's hearts turn to them,
    and provide them with produce,
    so that they may be thankful.
38 *Our Lord, You know well what we conceal and what we reveal:*
    nothing at all is hidden from God, on earth or in heaven.
39 *Praise be to God, who has granted me Ishmael and Isaac*
    in my old age: my Lord hears all requests!
40 *Lord, grant that I and my offspring may keep up the prayer.*
    Our Lord, accept my request.
41 *Our Lord, forgive me, my parents,*
    and the believers on the Day of Reckoning.‹

Here for the first time Abraham becomes a bearer of a
collective promise. As is prophesied to him in Genesis
15 for his descendants through Isaac, regarding their
fortunes and in particular their entry into the Promised Land, so in this prayer he asks for a leading position for his Arab descendants who are not at home in
a country flowing with milk and honey but in a bar-
ren place which, however, as the home of a monotheistic sanctuary, does have special dignity.

35 *Als Abraham sprach, Herr, mach diese Ortschaft sicher!*
   Und lass mich und meine Söhne den Götzendienst meiden!
36 *Herr, sie haben viele von den Menschen irregeführt.*
   Wenn nun einer mir folgt, gehört er zu mir.
   Und wenn sich einer widersetzt,
   nun, du bist vergebungsbereit und barmherzig!
37 *Herr, ich habe Leute aus meiner Nachkommenschaft angesie-*
   delt in einem Tal,
   in dem kein Getreide wächst,
   damit sie das Gebet verrichten.
   Mach, dass die Herzen der Menschen sich ihnen zuneigen,
   und beschere ihnen Früchte, auf dass sie dir dankbar seien!
38 *Herr, du weißt, was wir verbergen*
   und was wir bekanntmachen. Vor Gott ist nichts im Himmel
   oder auf Erden verborgen.
39 *Lob sei Gott, der mir trotz meines hohen Alters Ismael und*
   Isaak geschenkt hat.
   Mein Herr erhört das Gebet.
40 *Herr, mach, dass ich das Gebet verrichte und Leute aus meiner*
   Nachkommenschaft,
   Herr, und nimm mein Gebet an!
41 *Herr, vergib mir und meinen Eltern*
   und den Gläubigen am Tag, da abgerechnet wird.

Hier wird Abraham erstmals zum Träger einer kollektiven Verheißung: Wie ihm in Genesis 15 die Ge-
schicke und insbesondere der Einzug ins verheißene
Land für seine Nachkommen über Isaak prophe-
zeit werden, so erbittet er sich in diesem Gebet eine
Vorrangstellung für seine arabischen Nachkommen,
die zwar nicht in einem Land, »da Milch und Ho-
nig fließt«, sondern in einem unfruchtbaren Gebiet
zu Hause sind, das aber als Heimstatt eines monotheistischen Heiligtums besondere Dignität besitzt.

Already at the end of a previous conflict-pericope (Q 21:73), the descendants of Abraham were presented as »prophets and imams« who, among other things, were entrusted with the saying of prayers. Nicolai Sinai has highlighted this new awareness: »Q 14 now establishes a new reference to Mecca. At least some of the descendants of Abraham who were responsible for the saying of prayers do this in Mecca and thus represent the imams of the Meccans.«[71] Abraham and with him his faithful Arab descendants are therefore moved into a position relevant to the practice of the cult. Yet while this new connection of Abraham to the cultic center of the Kaaba in Mecca, as Sinai correctly stresses,[72] still belongs discursively to the politics of the winning over of the Meccans, Abraham's activity at the Kaaba in the Medina period becomes a new historical founding myth, in order that Abraham can now acquire an active role in the first practice of worship of the religious community. The winning over of the Meccans has to do with neutralizing the now well-established biblically inspired counter-history regarding the belonging of the community to the biblical *Banū Isrā'īl* (which seems to have been offensive to many people in Mecca) by emphasizing an Abrahamic local tradition and the connection to the progenitor of the Arabs, Ishmael.

Schon am Ende einer vorausgehenden Streitperikope (Q 21:73) waren Abrahams Nachkommen als »Propheten und Imame«, die unter anderem mit der Verrichtung des Gebets beauftragt sind, dargestellt worden. Nicolai Sinai hat diese neue Wahrnehmung hervorgehoben: »Q 14 stellt nun einen neuartigen Bezug zu Mekka her. Wenigstens einige der mit der Verrichtung des Gebets beauftragten Nachkommen Abrahams tun dies in Mekka und stellen insofern die Imame der Mekkaner dar«.[71] Abraham und mit ihm seine gläubigen arabischen Nachkommen rücken nun in eine kultisch relevante Position auf. Während aber diese neue Verbindung Abrahams zum Kultzentrum der Kaaba in Mekka, wie Sinai zu Recht betont,[72] diskursiv noch in die Politik der Gewinnung der Mekkaner gehört – es geht darum, die inzwischen etablierte, vielen Mekkanern offenbar anstößige biblisch inspirierte *counter-history* von der Zugehörigkeit der Gemeinde zu den biblischen *Banū Isrāʾīl* durch die Betonung einer abrahamitischen Lokaltradition und die Verbindung zu dem Stammvater der Araber, Ismael, zu neutralisieren – wird Abrahams Wirken an der Kaʿba in medinischer Zeit zu einem neuen Geschichtsgründungsmythos, so dass Abraham nun eine aktive Rolle bei der ersten Ausübung des Kultes zukommen kann.

The Medina Quran and Abraham's sacrifice:
Arabization of the biblical worldview

In Medina the Akedah story is read in a radically new way, without, however, being narrated again. The emigration of the community to Medina in the year 622 was a decisive turn through which the earlier Meccan pronouncements acquired a new religious-political dimension.[73] This in turn shocked the hitherto sought after »biblically shaped identity.« In Medina the Messenger and his audience are no longer isolated in a pagan/syncretistic context. They are now confronted with a Jewish community and no doubt also with individual religiously educated Christians who claimed for themselves biblical knowledge – which was, up to this point, considered to be a *universal* cultural good – as *their heritage*. In this context, the Jerusalem sanctuary must have appeared in a new light. For the early believers, it was the monotheistic center of the world, located in the Holy Land, in the area where the prophets had lived and proclaimed their message, in their spiritual homeland. On the part of the Jews, however, the Temple was laden with momentous and exclusively Jewish promises. Beyond biblical prophecies, it had acquired a rabbinic history of origin according to which it architecturally rested upon the foundations of that altar which Abraham and Isaac built together for their joint offering of sacrifice. For the Christians, the temple was detached from its topography. The church fathers gave it the

Der medinische Koran und das Abrahamsopfer: Arabisierung des biblischen Weltbilds

In Medina wird die Akedah-Geschichte radikal neu gelesen, ohne dass sie freilich noch einmal erzählt würde. Die Emigration der Gemeinde nach Medina im Jahr 622 hatte eine entscheidende Wende eingeleitet, durch die den älteren mekkanischen Verkündigungen eine neue – religionspolitische – Dimension zuwächst,[73] die die bis dahin angestrebte »biblisch geprägte Identität« erschüttert. In Medina stehen der Verkünder und seine Hörerschaft nicht mehr allein in einer paganen bis synkretistischen Umwelt, vielmehr sind sie jetzt mit einer jüdischen Gemeinde und wohl auch individuellen gebildeten Christen konfrontiert, die das bis dahin als *universales* Bildungsgut erachtete biblische Erbe als *ihr Erbe* für sich beanspruchen. Hier musste das Jerusalemer Heiligtum, das für die frühen Gläubigen der monotheistische Weltmittelpunkt gewesen war, gelegen im Heiligen Land, dem Wirkungsraum der Propheten, ihrer spirituellen Heimat, in einem neuen Licht erscheinen. Seitens der Juden war der Tempel »besetzt« mit schwerwiegenden exklusiv jüdischen Verheißungen. Über biblische Prophezeiungen hinaus hatte er außerdem eine rabbinische Gründungsgeschichte an sich gezogen, nach welcher er architektonisch auf dem Fundament jenes Altars aufruht, den Abraham zusammen mit Isaak zu ihrer gemeinsamen Darbringung des Opfers errichtet hatte. – Für die Christen war der Tempel aus sei-

new form of a spiritual building; yet, »Golgotha« also rests typologically on the foundations of Abraham's sacrifice. It was an edifice also built in a father-son synergy of God and Christ – the »wise architects of the faith.« What unites both traditions is apparently the belief that monotheistic holy places are of Abrahamic origin and that they owe their existence to a sacrifice which was offered synergistically by a father and a son.

It is in this context that the scene of sacrifice narrated above gains new significance for the Quranic community. The narrative in Q 37 is now, as we saw, »corrected« in its content through the addition of verse 102, that is, rewritten according to the rabbinic understanding into a synergistic story. In addition to this, it is now located in Mecca and through further steps upgraded to a crucially important event for the developing Islamic religion. As we saw, the connection of Abraham to Mecca before the *Hijra* was not yet a part of the community consensus; it was first introduced in the late Meccan sura Q 14, and this without any association with the *Akedah* or the *ḥajj*. Although he had already received an outstanding status in the late Meccan period (Abraham's readiness to offer his son as a sacrifice in Mecca, Q 37, had been celebrated as an exemplary proof of loyalty – one bearing, however, no consequences for the cult), it is probably due to the engagement with their

ner Topographie herausgelöst: Die Kirchenväter hatten ihm die neue Form eines spirituellen Bauwerks gegeben, aber auch »Golgata« ruhte typologisch auf den Grundfesten des Abrahamsopfers, es war ebenfalls in Vater-Sohn-Synergie, nun von Gott und Christus, den »weisen Architekten des Glaubens«, errichtet worden. Was beide Traditionen verbindet, ist offenbar die Überzeugung, dass monotheistische Heiligtümer abrahamitischen Ursprungs sind und dass sie sich einem von Vater und Sohn synergetisch dargebrachten Opfer verdanken.

Es ist in diesem Zusammenhang, dass die bereits erzählte Opferungsszene auch für die koranische Gemeinde neue Signifikanz gewinnt. Die Erzählung in Q 37 wird nun – wie wir sahen – zunächst durch den Zusatz von V. 102 inhaltlich »korrigiert«, das heißt nach dem rabbinischen Verständnis in eine Synergie-Geschichte umgeschrieben. Sie wird aber darüber hinaus in Mekka lokalisiert und in mehreren Schritten zu einer für die sich entwickelnde islamische Religion zentral wichtigen Begebenheit aufgewertet. Wie wir sahen, war die Verbindung Abrahams zu Mekka vor der Hidschra noch nicht Teil des gemeindlichen Konsenses, sondern wurde in der spätmekkanischen Sure Q 14 erst eingeführt, und auch dies noch ohne jede Assoziation zur Akedah oder dem *ḥadjdj*. Wenn ihm damit auch schon in Spätmekka ein herausragender Status zufällt, dürfte es doch erst der Auseinandersetzung mit den jüdischen Nachbarn geschuldet sein, dass Abrahams Op-

Jewish neighbors that Abraham's readiness to sacrifice his son is reclaimed by the Quranic community as a part of their local sacrifice-narrative. In Judaism, Abraham's readiness to sacrifice his son was of crucial significance being recognized as underlying the later Jewish sacrificial cult, and above all establishing the »merits of the fathers,« which privilege Judaism.[74] This cultic significance as the founding narrative for the practice of sacrifice is now also claimed by the Quranic community.

The ḥajj

This substantial upgrading – which is (as Snouck Hurgronje[75] has shown) preceded by a new appreciation of the great collective ritual of the *ḥajj* by the Medinan community – no longer happens through narrative additions to the story as originally told in its biblical sense. It no longer has to do with Abraham's willingness to offer his son as a sacrifice but rather with his sacrifice as an »archetypal scene« which, as it were, first establishes the institution of sacrifice. Abraham himself is raised to the status of the founder of the venerable institution of the *ḥajj*. This raising of his status, which has received little attention in research, is made possible by the common element of sacrifice as it is found both in the Akedah and in the *ḥajj*. Abraham, in the Bible the performer of sacrifice *par excellence*, now becomes the founder of a com-

ferbereitschaft, die in Mekka (Q 37) noch als beispiel-
hafter Treuebeweis, aber ohne Konsequenzen für den
Kult gefeiert worden war, angesichts ihrer sehr viel
höheren Bedeutung im Judentum – wo sie als dem
späteren jüdischen Opferkult als solchem zugrunde
liegend anerkannt wird und vor allem die das Judentum privilegierenden »Verdienste der Väter« begründet[74] – auch von der koranischen Gemeinde als Teil
ihrer lokalen Opfer-Geschichte reklamiert wird.

Der *ḥadjdj*

Diese substantielle Aufwertung, der – wie Snouck
Hurgronje[75] gezeigt hat – eine neue Wertschätzung
des großen kollektiven Rituals des *ḥadjdj* seitens der
medinischen Gemeinde vorausgeht, geschieht jedoch
nicht mehr durch narrative Ergänzungen zu der zunächst im biblischen Sinne erzählten Geschichte.
Es geht nicht mehr um Abrahams Opferwilligkeit,
sondern um sein Opfer als »Urszene«, die die Op-
ferinstitution gewissermaßen erst stiftet: Abraham
wird in den Rang des Begründers der altehrwürdigen Institution des *ḥadjdj* selbst erhoben. Diese in
der Forschung wenig beachtete Statuserhöhung wird
möglich durch das der Akedah und dem *ḥadjdj* gemeinsame Element des Opfers. Abraham, der Opfer-
darbringer par excellence, wird nun zum Stifter eines
komplexen Rituals, das im kollektiven Opfer kulmi-

plex ritual that culminates in a collective sacrifice.
The pilgrims consummate their multi-day rituals in
and around Mecca with the sacrificial feast, a cultic
slaughter, which is later also required of the head of a
household who remained home. It is a part of the hermeneutically motivated strategy of the biblicization
of Mecca that the old ritualistic acts of pilgrimage
(which were found extant)[76] were integrated – as rites
which Abraham had himself learned through divine
instruction (Q 2:128) – into the religious obligations
of the new religion. The performance of the *ḥajj* is
required of every believer who is »capable« to perform it (Q 3:97). The rites performed during the *ḥajj*,
however, acquire an entirely new interpretation as an
imitatio of Abraham. Abraham is assigned the Kaaba
as a holy place for the future Muslim worshippers –
those who practice the »circling around the Kaaba«
and the prayer rites (that is, »standing,« »bowing« and
»prostration«). He shall call for the pilgrimage which
culminates in sacrificing (here called euphemistically
»proclaim God's name over the livestock«) and ends
with circling around the Kaaba, Q 22:26–29:

26   *We showed Abraham the site of the Temple, saying, ›Do not
assign partners to Me. Purify My Temple for those who circle
around it, those who stand to pray, and those who bow and
prostrate themselves.*
27   *Proclaim the Pilgrimage to all people. They will come to you
on foot and on every kind of swift mount, emerging from every
deep mountain pass*

niert: Die Pilger beschließen ihre mehrtägigen Riten in und um Mekka mit dem Opferfest, einer kultischen Schlachtung, die später auch dem zu Hause gebliebenen Hausvater obliegt. Es ist Teil der hermeneutisch motivierten Strategie der »Biblisierung« Mekkas, dass die alten, von Muḥammad vorgefundenen Kulthandlungen der Wallfahrt[76] nun als Riten, die Abraham selbst durch göttliche Instruktion gelernt hat (Q 2:128), unter die Religionspflichten der neuen Religion integriert werden. Die Durchführung des *ḥadjdj* wird jedem Gläubigen auferlegt, der dazu »imstande ist« (Q 3:97). Die Riten erhalten dabei jedoch eine gänzlich neue Deutung, als *imitatio* Abrahams. Abraham erhält die Kaaba als Heiligtum zugewiesen für die dereinstigen muslimischen Kultteilnehmer – die den »Umlauf um die Kaaba« und die Gebetsriten, das heißt das »Stehen«, »Sich-Verneigen« und »Sich-Niederwerfen«, praktizieren. Er soll zur Wallfahrt aufrufen, die im Opfern (hier euphemistisch als »den Namen Gottes über dem Vieh ausrufen« angesprochen) kulminieren und mit einem Umlauf um die Kaaba enden soll (Q 22:26–29):

26 *Als wir Abraham die Stätte des Tempels als Heimstatt anwiesen: Geselle mir nichts bei, und reinige meinen Tempel für diejenigen, die den Umlauf vollziehen, die stehen und die sich verneigen und sich niederwerfen.*

27 *Rufe unter den Menschen zur Wallfahrt auf, dass sie zu dir kommen zu Fuß oder auf allerhand mageren Kamelen reitend, die aus lauter tief eingeschnittenen Passwegen hervorkommen.*

28   *to attain benefits and celebrate God's name, on specified days,*
      over the livestock He has provided for them — feed yourselves
      and the poor and unfortunate —
29   *so let the pilgrims perform their acts of cleansing, fulfil their*
      vows, and circle around the Ancient Temple.‹

This connection of Abraham with the *ḥajj*-sacrifice
has not to be regarded as another continuation of old
common Semitic forms of worship, as was formerly
held (based upon the common etymology of the Arabic *ḥajj* and the Hebrew *ḥagg*[77]), but as the breakthrough of late-antique forms of thought. Abraham,
the one who offers sacrifice, is typologically associated with an Arab ritual performance, in the center
of which stands sacrifice. In this way the *ḥajj*-ritu-
als, which were no longer convincing in their pagan
meaning, received new significance as actions initiated by Abraham.

The sacrifice

What kind of sacrifice is this? We know little about
the meaning of ancient Arab sacrifice. The *ḥajj* was,
before Islam, a festival for the changing of the seasons,[78] associated with ritual practices that, among
other things, were supposed to support the driving
out of the sun demons. The series of ascetic practices,
which had little verbal accompaniment and which

28 *Sie sollen dabei bezeugen, dass sie allerhand Nutzen davon*
   haben und an bestimmten Tagen den Namen Gottes über je-
   dem Stück Vieh ausrufen, das er ihnen beschert hat. Esst da-
   von und gebt dem Notleidenden und Armen davon.
29 *Hierauf sollen sie ihre körperliche Vernachlässigung abstellen,*
   ihre Gelübde erfüllen und den Umlauf um den altehrwürdigen
   Tempel vollziehen.

In dieser Verbindung Abrahams mit dem *ḥadjdj*-Op-
fer ist also nicht eine weitere Fortführung alter ge-
mein-semitischer Kultformen, wie man früher aufgrund der gemeinsamen Etymologie von arabisch
ḥadjdj und hebräisch *ḥagg* annahm,[77] zu sehen, sondern der Durchbruch spätantiker Denkformen. Abraham, der Opferer, wird typologisch assoziiert mit
demjenigen arabischen Zeremoniell, in dessen Zentrum das Opfer steht, so dass die in ihrer paganen
Bedeutung nicht mehr überzeugenden Riten neue
Signifikanz als von Abraham initiierte Handlungen
erhalten.

Das Opfer

Doch was für ein Opfer ist das? Wir wissen über
die Sinngebung des altarabischen Opfers wenig; der
ḥadjdj war vorislamisch ein Jahreszeitenwende-Fest,
verbunden mit rituellen Praktiken,[78] die unter anderem die Vertreibung der Sonnendämonen un-
terstützen sollten. Die sich über Tage erstreckende
Folge von kaum verbal begleiteten asketischen Prak-

were carried out over several days at different cultic places, culminated in a communal sacrifice. This was an important moment in establishing coherence for society. Its retention in the new monotheistic context might suggest that the turn from collective rituality to personal piety, which was achieved elsewhere, was not consistently carried through in Islam. This impression is deceptive, however, because the Quran does achieve, with its new overall-interpretation of the *ḥajj* (as an institution of Abraham, Q 22:26 f.) a decisive sublimation of the rituals, and thus a step from a form of religion based on the observance of ritual – which Guy Stroumsa calls »civil religion« – to a »communitarian religion«, in which the faith of the individual is paramount. Indeed, the sacrificing of animals does not retain any symbolic significance – neither in the sense of the establishment of collective coherence nor in a theological sense. While the act of sacrifice is explicitly instructed in Q 2:27 as an integral act of the *ḥajj*, it is nevertheless also demythified into an act of piety, reinterpreted as *taqwā*, »fear of God«. This new understanding is made clear in Q 22:36 f.:

36   *We have made camels part of God's sacred rites for you.*
     There is much good in them for you,
     so invoke God's name over them […].
37   *It is neither their meat nor their blood that reaches God*
     but your piety. […]

tiken an verschiedenen Kultorten kulminierte in einem gemeinschaftlichen Opfer, das ein wichtiges Moment der Kohärenzstiftung der Gesellschaft war. Seine Beibehaltung im neuen monotheistischen Kontext könnte suggerieren, dass die anderswo vollzogene Wende von kollektiver Ritualität zu persönlicher Frömmigkeit im Islam nicht konsequent durchgemacht worden ist. Dieser Eindruck täuscht jedoch, denn der Koran nimmt mit seiner neuen *overall*-Deutung des *ḥadjdj* als einer Stiftung Abrahams (Q 22:26 f.) eine entscheidende Sublimierung der Riten vor, also den Schritt von einer auf der Einhaltung des Ritus beruhenden Religionsform – Guy Stroumsas »ziviler Religion« – hin zu einer »kommunitären Religion«, in der der Glaube des Einzelnen ausschlaggebend ist. Denn den Tieropfern kommt laut Koran keine symbolische Bedeutung zu, weder im Sinne der Stiftung kollektiver Kohärenz noch etwa theologisch. Die Opferhandlung selbst wird zwar in Q 2:27 als integrale Handlung des *ḥadjdj* angewiesen, sie wird aber zugleich entmythisiert, zu einem Akt der Frömmigkeit, *taqwā* (»Gottesfurcht«), umgedeutet. Q 22:36 f. macht dieses neue Verständnis klar:

36 *Die Opferkamele haben wir euch zu Kultsymbolen Gottes gemacht. Ihr habt an ihnen Gutes. Sprecht den Namen Gottes über ihnen aus […].*
37 *Weder ihr Fleisch noch ihr Blut wird zu Gott gelangen, wohl aber die Gottesfurcht von euch. […]*

Replacing the establishment of collective coherence through the pagan cult is the personal merit of the individual, his relationship of piety, *eusebeia*, from which he carries out the slaughter. Furthermore, and in a manner also characteristic of late antiquity, the act of slaughtering has merit as a means to charitable activity, namely, the feeding of the poor. At the same time, the sacrifice is clearly removed from the Judeo-Christian understanding as an act of a collectively relevant atonement for guilt, it is emptied of every mythical dimension – being no more than an expression of the pious attitude of the individual – of his fear of God, *taqwā*. With regard to the Quran, one is thus entitled to speak of an »end of sacrifice« in the sense suggested by Stroumsa, that is, the relocation of an act which affirms the collective identity to an individual act of piety.

Nevertheless, the radical reinterpretation of the *ḥajj* – the anchoring of local Arab tradition (still imprinted with pagan traits) in the life of the most important biblical patriarch – remains a drastic religious and political step which requires an explanation. The Islamic tradition and, in its wake, individual Western researchers ignore this break. They proceed from a »faith of Abraham« assumed to have been already widespread in Arabia and with which the Quran simply establishes connections. This contradicts, however, the image of Abraham during the Meccan proclamation where Abraham was still per-

Was an die Stelle der Stiftung kollektiver Kohärenz im paganen Kult getreten ist, ist ein persönliches Verdienst des Einzelnen, seine Bezeigung von Gottesfurcht (*eusebeia*), aus der heraus er die Schlachtung vornimmt. Weiterhin besitzt der Akt der Schlachtung Verdienstlichkeit als Möglichkeit zu einem – gleichfalls für die Spätantike charakteristischen – karitativen Handeln: zu Armenspeisungen. Gleichzeitig wird das Opfer aber auch eindeutig von dem jüdisch-christlichen Verständnis als Akt kollektiv relevanter Schuldtilgung abgehoben, denn es erscheint jeder mythischen Dimension entleert, einzig als Ausdruck der frommen Gesinnung des Einzelnen, seiner Gottesfurcht, *taqwā*. Man kann für den Koran selbst also durchaus ein »Ende des Opfers« im Stroumsaschen Sinne, das heißt die Verlagerung eines kollektive Identität affirmierenden Aktes hin zu einem individuellen Akt der Frömmigkeit, geltend machen.

Dennoch bleibt die radikale Umdeutung des *ḥadjdj*, die Verankerung der so deutlich pagane Züge tragenden arabischen Lokaltradition in die Vita des bedeutendsten biblischen Erzvaters, religionspolitisch ein einschneidender Schritt, der nach Erklärung verlangt. Die islamische Tradition und in ihrem Gefolge auch einzelne westliche Forscher ignorieren diesen Einschnitt. Sie gehen von einer bereits in Arabien verbreiteten »Religion Abrahams« aus, an die der Koran nur anknüpfe. Das widerspricht jedoch dem Bild Abrahams während der mekkanischen Verkündigung, wo Abraham noch als einer der biblischen

ceived as one of the biblical men of God of the type of Noah (Q 37:83) whom it would have been difficult to associate with the ancient Arab ritual of the *ḥajj* celebrating the changing of the seasons. Nicolai Sinai, who has documented the development, concludes that a presence of Abraham and his descendants in Mecca are indeed mentioned in the late Meccan sura Q 14:35 ff.; yet this is connected with neither the *ḥajj* nor the *Aqedah*: »The fact that all of these ideas become visible only gradually in the Quran suggests that they did not represent a general consensus of the Meccan society.«[79] If Abraham had already been known to have been involved in the *ḥajj*-ritual this would have certainly been mentioned in Q 14 which brings him into connection with Mecca. One may therefore presume, as has already been proposed by Snouck Hurgronje,[80] that it was in Medina that the ritual for the changing of the seasons[81] first received its new interpretation as a memorial of a salvation-historical event, namely Abraham's establishment of the monotheistic pilgrimage. Should it therefore be discarded as a merely political maneuver by Muhammad, as Hurgronje suggests? A glance at the debates of the Medinan community with their Jewish neighbors suggests another explanation.

Gottesmänner »vom Schlage des Noah« (Q 37:88) wahrgenommen worden war, der mit einem Szenario wie dem altarabischen Jahreszeitenwende-Ritual des *ḥadjdj* schwer zu assoziieren gewesen wäre. Nicolai Sinai, der die Entwicklung dokumentiert hat, kommt zu dem Schluss, dass eine Präsenz Abrahams bzw. seiner Nachkommen in Mekka zwar in der spätmekkanischen Sure Q 14:35 ff. zur Sprache kommt, diese sich aber weder mit dem *ḥadjdj* noch mit der Aqedah verbindet: »Die Tatsache, dass all diese Vorstellungen erst nach und nach im Koran sichtbar werden, deutet darauf hin, dass es sich hierbei keineswegs um einen allgemeinen Konsens der mekkanischen Gesellschaft gehandelt haben dürfte.«[79] Wäre Abraham bereits früher als in den *ḥadjdj*-Ritus involviert bekannt gewesen, hätte dies gewiss in seiner ihn mit Mekka verbindenden Geschichte in Q 14 Niederschlag gefunden. Man hat also, wie von Snouck Hurgronje bereits verfochten,[80] davon auszugehen, dass der Schritt der Neuinterpretation eines Jahreszeitenwende-Ritus[81] in die Erinnerung an eine heilsgeschichtliche Begebenheit, nämlich Abrahams Stiftung der monotheistischen Wallfahrt, erst in Medina vollzogen wurde. Kann er deswegen aber einfach wie bei Hurgronje als ein politischer Schachzug Muhammads abgetan werden? Ein Blick auf die Debatten der medinischen Gemeinde mit ihren jüdischen Nachbarn legt eine andere Erklärung nahe.

The topographic typology of
Jerusalem – Mecca

This debate is concerned with the status of the sanctuaries. The fact that Abraham can take on the role of the founder of the Meccan rituals is owed to a typological reinterpretation of the Kaaba as such which apparently still precedes Q 22:27. It is already reflected clearly in the Quranic instruction to change the *qibla* from the Jerusalem temple to the Kaaba which is traditionally connected with the outcome of the Battle of Badr in the second year of the Islamic calendar. The typological reinterpretation of the Kaaba seems to presuppose the Jewish tradition of the building of the temple in Jerusalem on the foundation of the altar which Abraham erected for the sacrifice of his son. The Medinan addition to the Meccan Aqedah-narrative, which connects the event to a *ḥajj*-ritual (Q 37:102), had already typologically identified Mecca as the location of the Aqedah. As someone who had already been involved in the *ḥajj* ceremonies, Abraham becomes plausible in his role as the founder of the Arab cult. His participation in the *ḥajj*, as mentioned in Q 37:102, now reads like an embedding of the Aqedah-narrative into Arabian local history: »When he, together with his son reached the phase of the *saʿy* (a ritual parcours between two minor sanctuaries which precedes the sacrifice), Abraham said to him, … I will sacrifice you.« The verses

Die topographische Typologie
Jerusalem – Mekka

In dieser Debatte geht es um den Status der Heiligtümer. Denn dass Abraham die Rolle des Stifters
der Riten übernehmen kann, verdankt sich offenbar einer Q 22:27 noch vorausgehenden typologischen Neudeutung der Kaaba als solcher. Sie schlägt
sich bereits deutlich nieder in der koranischen An-
weisung zur *qibla*-Änderung vom Jerusalemer Tempel zur Kaaba, die traditionell mit dem Ausgang der
Schlacht von Badr im Jahr 2 der Hidschra verbunden
wird. Die typologische Neudeutung der Kaaba lehnt
sich an die in der jüdischen Tradition aufrechterhal-
tene Errichtung des Jerusalemer Tempels an, der als
auf den Fundamenten des von Abraham zur Opferung seines Sohnes errichteten Altars basierend vorgestellt wird. Schon der medinische Zusatz zu der
mekkanischen Akedah-Geschichte, der das Ereignis
in das *ḥadjdj*-Ritual einfügte (Q 37:102), hatte Mekka
typologisch als den Ort der Akedah identifiziert. Als
jemand, der bereits an den Zeremonien beteiligt gewesen war, wird Abraham in seiner Rolle als der
Gründer des arabischen Kultes plausibel. Seine in Q
37:102 erwähnte Teilnahme am *ḥadjdj* liest sich nun
wie eine Einbettung der Akedah-Geschichte in die
arabische Lokalgeschichte: Als er mit dem Sohn die
Phase des *sa'y* (eines Parcours zwischen zwei kleinen
Heiligtümern, der dem Opfer vorausgeht) erreicht
hatte, sprach Abraham zu ihm, »[…] ich soll dich op-

Q 2:125–129, which seal the new role of Abraham as the founder of the sanctuary, read:

125 *We made the Temple a resort and a sanctuary for people, saying, ›Take the spot where Abraham stood as your place of prayer.‹ We commanded Abraham and Ishmael: ›Purify My Temple for those who walk round it, those who stay there, and those who bow and prostrate themselves in worship.‹*

126 *Abraham said, ›My Lord, make this land secure and provide with produce those of its people who believe in God and the Last Day.‹ God said, ›As for those who disbelieve, I will grant them enjoyment for a short while and then subject them to the torment of the Fire – an evil destination.‹*

127 *As Abraham and Ishmael built up the foundations of the Temple [they prayed], ›Our Lord, accept [this sacrifice?] from us. You are the All Hearing, the All Knowing.*

128 *Our Lord, make us devoted to You; make our descendants into a community devoted to You. Show us how to worship and accept our repentance, for You are the Ever Relenting, the Most Merciful.*

129 *Our Lord, make a messenger of their own rise up from among them, to recite Your revelations to them, teach them the Scripture and wisdom, and purify them: You are the Mighty, the Wise.‹*

fern«. Die Verse Q 2:125–129, die Abrahams neue Rolle als Stifter des Heiligtums besiegeln, lauten:

125 *Als wir den Tempel zu einer Stätte der Einkehr für die Men-schen und zu einem Ort der Sicherheit machten:* »Nehmt euch den Standplatz Abrahams zur Gebetsstätte!« *Und wir verpflichteten Abraham und Ismael:* »Reinigt meinen Tempel für diejenigen, die den Umlauf vollziehen, und für die, die sich dem Gottesdienst widmen, und für die, die sich verneigen und niederwerfen!«

126 *Als dann Abraham sprach:* »Herr, mach dies zu einer sicheren Ortschaft und beschere ihren Einwohnern Früchte – denen von ihnen, die an Gott und den Jüngsten Tag glauben!« *Gott sprach:* »Wer aber ungläubig ist, dem gewähre ich ein wenig Genuss. Hierauf zwinge ich ihn in die Strafe des Höllen-feuers – welch ein schlimmes Ende.«

127 *Als Abraham die Grundmauern des Tempels aufrichtete, sprachen er und Ismael:*
»Unser Herr, nimm [unser Opfer?] von uns an! Du bist der Hörende, der Sehende.

128 *Unser Herr, gib, dass wir dir ergeben sind und mache aus unseren Nachkommen eine dir ergebene Ge-meinde* [ummatan muslimatan].
Weise uns in unsere Riten ein und wende dich uns zu! Du bist der, der sich zukehrt, der Barmherzige.

129 *Unser Herr, lass unter ihnen einen Gesandten aus ihrer Mitte auftreten,*
der ihnen deine Zeichen [Verse] *vorträgt und sie die Schrift und die Weisheit lehrt und sie läutert.*
Du bist der Mächtige, der Weise.«

As Joseph Witztum has persuasively shown, there is a Quranic restaging of an episode in the life of Abraham here, a theme which had acquired many layers of interpretation in late antiquity.[82] Initially, a simple »material typology« is at work, at the center of which is the building activity of the two patriarchs. Josephus had already credited Isaac with a role in the construction of the altar on which he was to be sacrificed.[83] Yet the participation of the son, as Witztum demonstrates, is underscored even stronger in Christian traditions. Various Syrian and Greek homilies from the fourth and fifth centuries show this; they interpret the story christologically: God the Father and God the Son, the »wise architects of the faith,« together build the altar upon which the redeeming sacrifice of the Son is to be offered. In the Quranic text no altar is mentioned, what matters is the construction of a concrete holy place. Nevertheless, the prayer »for acceptance« in verse 127 should point to the acceptance of a sacrifice.[84] In addition, as Nicolai Sinai suggests, »against the background of the Jewish idea, that the Jerusalem temple was built on the site of Abraham's sacrifice, the call *wa-ttakhidhū min maqāmi Ibrāhīma muṣallan* (Q 2:125) could have had the original meaning of ›take the place as the place of prayer where Abraham stood when he wanted to sacrifice his son.‹«[85] Q 2:127–9 deals most importantly with the typological rendering of the Jerusalem temple through the image of the Kaaba, in the sense of a cultic center. Initially, this cult is to include the rituals.

Wie Joseph Witztum überzeugend gezeigt hat,[82] liegt hier eine koranische Reinszenierung der in der Spätantike vielschichtig gewordenen Vita Abrahams vor. Dabei ist zunächst eine einfache materiale Typologie wirksam, in deren Zentrum die Bauaktivität der beiden Patriarchen steht. Bereits Josephus lässt Isaak am Bau des Altars beteiligt sein, auf dem er geopfert werden soll.[83] Doch steht die Beteiligung des Sohnes an gerade diesem Bau, wie Witztum belegen kann, noch stärker im Mittelpunkt christlicher Traditionen, wie verschiedene syrische und griechische Homilien aus dem 4. und 5. Jahrhundert zeigen, die die Begebenheit christologisch interpretieren: Gott Vater und Sohn, die »weisen Architekten des Glaubens«, bauen gemeinsam den Altar, auf dem das erlösende Sohnesopfer dargebracht werden soll. – Im koranischen Text wird zwar kein Altar erwähnt, hier geht es um den Bau eines konkreten Heiligtums, doch könnte das Gebet »um Annahme« in V. 127 auf die eines Opfers zielen.[84] Außerdem könnte – wie Nicolai Sinai vorschlägt – »vor dem Hintergrund, dass der Jerusalemer Tempel am Ort von Abrahams Opfer errichtet ist, der Aufruf *wa-ttakhidhū min maqāmi Ibrāhīma muṣallan* (Q 2:125) die ursprüngliche Bedeutung ›Nehmt euch den Ort, an dem Abraham stand, als er das Sohnesopfer vollziehen wollte, zum Gebetsort‹ gehabt haben.«[85] Es geht in Q 2:127–9 zentral um die typologische Abbildung des Jerusalemer Heiligtums durch die Kaaba im Sinne eines Zentrums des Kultes. Dieser Kult soll zunächst die Riten

In the distant future, however, it is to take the form
of a verbal service. The prayer is a *vaticinatio ex eventu*:
the promised messenger who will teach the scriptures
and wisdom has already come with the Prophet Muhammad. The prayer of Abraham has been compared
with the temple consecration prayer of Solomon and
has thus been apostrophized as the »prayer of the
consecration of the Kaaba«. In fact, the Kaaba, »the
Temple,« in this context is the authentic antitype to
which the Jerusalem Temple corresponds as the *typos*.

The innovation apparent in Q 2:124–129 – the
establishment of the Kaaba by Abraham and Ishmael, their joint prayer for the sacred integrity of the
Kaaba – thus reflects the typology between two holy
places. It is a stop on the way of the superimposition
of Mecca over Jerusalem (which was previously central to the community) explicitly documented in the
Quran by the *qibla*-change. The involvement of Ishmael in the Kaaba-founding can be considered an in-
dication of the Arabicization of the tradition. Insofar
as he is known to be the genealogical father of the
Arabs, Ishmael is apparently needed here as the son
who was involved in the sacrifice. Yet, later in the
Quran he does not have a position comparable to the
Jewish Isaac.

The verse about the coming of a prophet of scripture can only be read as a testimony to a form of worship (now also verbal), which was gradually developing under the new conditions of a preeminence given
to Mecca over Jerusalem. In Abraham's prayer, the

einschließen, in der ferneren Zukunft aber auch die Form eines Wortgottesdienstes annehmen. Das Gebet ist eine *vaticinatio ex eventu*: Der erflehte Gesandte, der Schrift und Weisheit lehren wird, ist mit dem Propheten Muḥammad schon gekommen. Das Gebet Abrahams ist mit dem Tempelweihe-Gebet Salomos verglichen worden und daher als Kaaba-Weihegebet apostrophiert worden. In der Tat ist die Kaaba, »der Tempel«, hier der eigentliche Antitypus, dem als Typus der Jerusalemer Tempel entspricht.

Die sich in Q 2:124–129 abzeichnende Innovation – die Errichtung der Kaaba durch Abraham und Ismael, ihr gemeinsames Gebet um die sakrale Integrität der Kaaba – spiegelt also die Typologie zwischen zwei Heiligtümern. Sie ist eine Station auf dem Weg der Überlagerung des vorher für die Gemeinde zentralen Jerusalem durch Mekka, die durch die Qibla-Änderung auch koranisch dokumentiert ist. Die Beteiligung Ismaels an der Kaaba-Gründung kann als ein Indiz der Arabisierung der Tradition gelten – Ismael wird hier offenbar, insofern er genealogisch als Stammvater der Araber gilt, als der in das Opfer involvierte Sohn »gebraucht« –; er hat späterhin im Koran aber keine dem jüdischen Isaak vergleichbare Position.

Der Vers über das Kommen eines Schriftpropheten kann nur als Zeugnis für den sich sukzessiv herausbildenden, nun auch verbalen Kultus unter Vorrangstellung Mekkas vor Jerusalem gelesen werden. In Abrahams Gebet wird das wichtige Vorrecht Je-

important privilege of Jerusalem – the place of the origin of scripture and of service to the word of God (Isaiah 2:3, »For out of Zion shall go the law, and the word of the Lord from Jerusalem«) – is transferred to Mecca. What is true there for Jerusalem shall now also apply to Mecca. With the appearance of Muhammad there, the Messenger of scripture and God's word (as invoked by Abraham) had now really come. Mecca is thus the »first House of God« – as it says in 3:96 –, that is, the holy place which is older than Jerusalem because it already goes back to Abraham. In this process of the biblicization of Mecca – the biblicization of its form of worship and history – no other character is as substantially involved as Abraham.

If one considers the structural similarities of the three father-son synergies of late antiquity with regard to the establishment of the respective sanctuaries (as addressed above), it might initially appear as though Ishmael was involved in the founding of the Meccan Kaaba as Isaac was involved in the founding of the Jerusalem sacrificial site of Moriah (which is identified with the foundation of the Jewish temple), or as Christ was involved in the founding of the place of sacrifice at Golgotha (to follow the allegorical Christian homilies). The comparison is, however, not entirely accurate: the Quran lacks a crucial dimension in the father-son synergism that is owed to, in the other two religions, the theologically heavily charged idea of sacrifice. In Judaism, the temple cult (which is central for the identity of antique and

rusalems, Ursprungsort der Schrift und des Wortgottesdienstes zu sein (Jesaja 2,3: »Denn von Zion wird ausgehen Lehre und das Wort Gottes von Jerusalem«), auf Mekka übertragen. Was dort für Jerusalem gilt, soll nun auch für Mekka zutreffen, wo mit Muḥammads Auftreten der von Abraham erflehte Verkünder von Schrift und Gotteswort nun wirklich gekommen ist. Mekka ist also das »erste Gotteshaus«, wie es in Q 3:96 heißt, das heißt das gegenüber Jerusalem ältere Heiligtum, weil es bereits auf Abraham zurückgeht. An dieser Biblisierung Mekkas, seines Kultus und seiner Geschichte, ist keine Figur so substantiell beteiligt wie Abraham.

Beachtet man die Strukturähnlichkeiten der drei in der Spätantike diskutierten Vater-Sohn-Synergismen bei der Errichtung des jeweiligen Heiligtums, so könnte es zunächst so scheinen, als sei Ismael an der mekkanischen Kaabagründung beteiligt, wie Isaak an der Gründung der Jerusalemer Opferstätte von Moria beteiligt ist, die später Grundlage des jüdischen Tempels wurde, oder wie – den allegorisierenden christlichen Homilien zufolge – Christus an der Gründung der Opferstätte von Golgatha beteiligt war. Der Vergleich trifft aber nicht vollständig zu: Im Koran fehlt dem Vater-Sohn-Synergismus eine entscheidende Dimension, die sich in den beiden anderen Religionen dem theologisch schwerwiegenden Opfergedanken verdankt. Im Judentum wird durch das Abrahamsopfer der für die Identität des antiken

late antique Judaism) is prefigured by Abraham's sacrifice. At the same time, Abraham and Isaac establish the basis for the thesaurus of God's loving care to their descendants, the *zekhut avot*. In Christianity, the Aqedah prefigures the atoning sacrifice of the Christian passion. Such a dimension is not connected to Abraham's sacrifice, as a prefiguration of the sacrifice which was offered within the *ḥajj*. The *ḥajj*-ritual focuses only on the one who offers sacrifice and the sacrificial animal that is offered as a substitute. It does not focus on the privileges that are acquired through the sacrifice, and even less so on the aspect of an atoning reparation provided by the sacrifice. In this sense, it is a case of the demythification of already extant traditions.[86] Nevertheless, the new construction of the central sanctuary, which is achieved through these »verbal-semantic« typologies, appears as more than a re-enactment, namely, the fulfillment of the meaningfulness of the father-son synergy which was promised with the Aqedah.

A new »Abrahamic religion«: Religious practice as a precursor of scripture

If one asks what is new in the special positioning of the person of Abraham in Islam vis-à-vis the preceding reception of Abraham, the answer that comes to mind is the new conception of sacrifice. The understanding of Abraham (obviously established through

und noch spätantiken Judentums zentrale Tempelkult präfiguriert. Zugleich stiften Abraham und Isaak die Grundlage für den Thesaurus göttlicher Zuwendung an das Kollektiv ihrer Nachkommen, die *zekhut avot*. Im Christentum präfiguriert die Aqedah das Sühneopfer der christlichen Passion. Eine solche Dimension verbindet sich mit dem Abrahamsopfer als Präfiguration des innerhalb des *ḥadjdj* dargebrachten Opfers nicht. Der *ḥadjdj*-Ritus fokussiert nur den Opfernden und das als Ersatz dargebrachte Opfertier, nicht aber die mit dem Opfer erkauften Privilegien und noch weniger den Aspekt der mit dem Opfer erbrachten Sühneleistung – ein Fall von Entmythisierung vorgefundener Traditionen.[86] Gleichwohl scheint die durch diese »verbal-semantischen« Typologien erreichte Neu-Konstruktion des zentralen Heiligtums mehr als ein *re-enactment*, nämlich vielmehr die Erfüllung der mit der Akedah verheißenen Sinnhaftigkeit der Vater-Sohn-Synergie zu sein.

Eine neue »abrahamitische Religion«:
Der Kult als Vorstufe der Schrift

Fragt man nach dem Neuen, das die besondere Positionierung der Person Abrahams im Islam in vorausgehende Abraham-Rezeption eingebracht hat, so fällt zunächst die neue Konzeption des Opfers auf. Die in der Auseinandersetzung mit den Juden von

the engagement with the Jews of Medina) as a central memorial figure in the complex ceremony of the *ḥajj* is certainly the most visible manifestation of his presence in Islamic piety. With the integration of ancient Arab forms of religious worship into his biblical *vita*, Abraham comes back into view as a founder of a cult, and thus as the one who offers sacrifice, as he was already depicted in the biblical context (cf. Gen. 12:6–8, 13:18). The *ḥajj*-sacrifice, which was already practiced before the proclamation of the Quran, is adopted – under the new perspective of a *imitatio* of Abraham into the central rituals of the new religion. It thus receives a biblical aura. It is an organic continuation of a local tradition with an important theological modification. The Islamic sacrifice is a divested sacrifice; it is divested of every mythical dimension that may be established through blood (as this is understood elsewhere for the purging of sins). The offering of this sacrifice is above all relevant as an expression of personal piety.

The raising of Abraham to the status of a founder of a religious cult was not an isolated step. On the contrary, it was embedded in a dispute about sanctuaries. A topographic typology – as undertaken in the rabbinic tradition (which anchored the Temple Mount in the patriarchal history) – also allowed for the inclusion of the Kaaba in the same narrative. According to this new connection, Mecca is – as Jerusalem was before – the center of the world, the place where the prayers of the devout converge, the *qibla*.

Medina etablierte Wahrnehmung Abrahams als zentraler Erinnerungsfigur bei der komplexen Zeremonie des *ḥadjdj* ist gewiss die augenfälligste Manifestation seiner Präsenz in der islamischen Frömmigkeit. Mit der Einbindung altarabischer kultischer Praktiken in seine biblische Vita rückt Abraham als Kultstifter und damit Opfer-Darbringer, der er bereits im biblischen Kontext war (vergleiche Genesis 12,6–8; 13,18) wieder in den Blick. Das vor der Koranverkündigung bereits praktizierte *ḥadjdj*-Opfer wird so unter dem neuen Vorzeichen einer *imitatio* Abrahams unter die zentralen Riten der neuen Religion aufgenommen. Es erhält damit eine biblische Aura. Es ist organische Fortführung einer Lokaltradition, doch mit bedeutender theologischer Modifikation – denn das islamische Opfer ist ein jeder mythischen Dimension, die durch das anderswo purgierend wahrgenommene Blut gestiftet wird, entkleidetes Opfer, dessen Ausführung vor allem als Ausdruck persönlicher Frömmigkeit relevant ist.

Die Erhebung Abrahams in den Rang eines Kultstifters war kein isolierter Schritt. Sie ist vielmehr eingebettet in eine Auseinandersetzung um die Heiligtümer. Eine in der rabbinischen Tradition vorgenommene topographische Typologie, die den Tempelberg in der Patriarchengeschichte verankerte, ermöglicht auch die Inklusion der Kaaba in dieselbe Geschichte. Dieser neuen Verbindung zufolge ist Mekka – wie früher Jerusalem – der Mittelpunkt der Welt, der Ort, an dem die Gebete der Frommen

Arabia thus becomes a part of the »Holy Land,« a part of the *topographia sacra*. This is not as a mere annex, however. The hub, the center of gravity of the prayers, is relocated to Mecca, which, as a »type« of Jerusalem, will now take, as suggested by the ranking order as »first temple« in Q 3:96, the most important place.

The newly emerging religion consists not just in its ritual practices, however, but above all in the way in which it ›re-presents‹ Holy Scripture, bringing it, as it were, into the present. It is only logical that Abraham, after the death of the Prophet, finds a place in the daily prayer which is now fixed in its procedure and formulation. Besides the Prophet Muhammad himself, the blessings which are to be articulated at the end of the ritual prayer apply to only one of his prophetic predecessors: Abraham. The text at the end of the prayer says: *Allāhumma bārik ʿalā Muḥammad ka-mā bārakta ʿalā Ibrāhīm. Allāhumma bārik ʿalā āli Muḥammad ka-mā bārakta ʿalā āli Ibrāhīm* »God, bless Muhammad as you have blessed Abraham. God, bless the family of Muhammad as you have blessed the family of Abraham.« Abraham is remembered here as one who has been blessed; it is a reminiscence of his distinction with a eulogy that he received because of his readiness to offer his son as a sacrifice. It corresponds to the biblical promise of blessing which, in the Genesis account, follows the divine recognition of Abraham's faithfulness: »in your offspring shall all the nations of the earth be blessed, because

konvergieren, die *qibla*. Arabien wird damit Teil des »Heiligen Landes«, der *topographia sacra*, jedoch nicht als bloßer Annex, vielmehr wird der Mittelpunkt, das Gravitationszentrum der Gebete selbst, nach Mekka verlegt, das als Typus von Jerusalem, wie es die Rangordnung als »erster Tempel« in Q 3:96 nahelegt, jetzt den bedeutendsten Rang einnehmen soll.

Aber die neu entstehende Religion ist nicht nur Ritenvollzug, sie ist vor allem Vergegenwärtigung der Schrift. Es ist nur konsequent, dass Abraham nach dem Tode des Propheten auch in das tägliche Gebet Einzug hält, das nun in seinem Ablauf und seiner Formulatur festgelegt wird. Die am Schluss zu artikulierenden Segenswünsche des Ritualgebets gelten außer dem Propheten Muḥammad selbst nur einem einzigen seiner prophetischen Vorläufer: Abraham. Es heißt am Ende des Gebets: *Allāhumma bārik ʿalā Muḥammad ka-mā bārakta ʿalā Ibrāhīm. Allāhumma bārik ʿalā āli Muḥammad ka-mā bārakta ʿalā āli Ibrāhīm* (»Gott, segne Muḥammad, wie du gesegnet hast Abraham. Gott, segne die Angehörigen Muḥammads, wie Du gesegnet hast die Angehörigen Abrahams«). Abraham wird hier in Erinnerung gerufen als derjenige, dem bereits Segen zuteil wurde, eine Reminiszenz seiner Auszeichnung mit einer Eulogie, die er für seine Opferbereitschaft erhielt. Sie entspricht der biblischen Segensverheißung, die im Genesisbericht auf die göttliche Anerkennung von Abrahams Treue folgt: »Durch deine Nachkommen sollen alle Völker der Erde gesegnet werden, weil du auf meine Stimme

you have obeyed my voice« (Gen 22:18). He is therefore to be recalled in the memory of the congregation as the one whom God has blessed or will bless
repeatedly, Q 37:108–9: »We let him be praised by
succeeding generations: ›Peace be upon Abraham!‹«
The family of both prophets (in the sense of Q 3:33
this would be above all the spiritual relatives) should
also receive such blessings: as the righteous among
the followers of Abraham in history, so now those of
Muhammad in the present. Abraham's piety and his
sacrifice –, which underlies the religious practice of
the two other religions in the form of a verbal sacrifice, a liturgy, or a symbolic act of sacrifice –, di-
verge in the Islamic tradition. In the Islamic prayer,
the concept of sacrifice is not remembered. In that the
prayer is oriented towards Mecca, however, Abraham's achievement, as the originator of a *cultus*, as
the one who had first introduced Mecca as a place of
worship to the world of late antiquity, remains unmistakably present. But sacrifice is no longer, as in
pre-Islam, the centerpiece of the *cultus*; on the contrary, this position is held by prayer. At the end of the
development, there is not a symbolic re-enactment of
the sacrifice, but a shared presence of Abraham and
the Prophet Muhammad as »Imams« (Q 21:73). This
draws them out of the hitherto only typological relationship and involves both of them together in a new
liturgical synergy: Abraham, as the founder of the
»antique« ritual religious practice, and Muhammad,
as the consummator of »late-antique« verbal religious

gehört hast« (Genesis 22,18). Er sollte daher im Gedächtnis der Gemeinde erinnert werden als derjenige, den Gott gesegnet hat oder immer wieder seg-
net (Q 37:108–109): »wir ließen den Späteren den
Spruch zurück ›Segen sei über Abraham‹«. Auch die
Angehörigen – im Sinne von Q 3:33 wären dies vor
allem die »spirituellen Angehörigen«, die Anhänger
– beider Propheten sollen einen solchen Segen erhalten, wie die Gerechten unter den Anhängern Abrahams in der Geschichte, so nun diejenigen Muḥammads in der Gegenwart. Abrahams Frömmigkeit und
das Abrahamsopfer, das – umgewandelt in ein ver-
bales Opfer, eine Liturgie, bzw. in eine symbolische
Opferhandlung – dem Kult der beiden anderen Religionen zugrundeliegt, treten in der islamischen Tradition auseinander. Im islamischen Gebet wird der
Opfergedanke nicht erinnert. Aber da das Gebet in
Richtung Mekka ausgerichtet ist, bleibt Abrahams
Leistung als Kultstifter, der Mekka als Kultort erst in
die Welt der Spätantike eingeführt hat, unverkennbar gegenwärtig. Dennoch ist das Opfer nicht mehr
wie im Vorislam das Herzstück des Kultes, das ist
vielmehr das Gebet. Am Ende der Entwicklung steht
nicht eine symbolische Reinszenierung des Opfers,
sondern eine gemeinsame Präsenz Abrahams und des
Propheten Muḥammad als »Imame« (Q 21:73), die sie
aus dem bis dahin nur typologischen Verhältnis löst
und sie beide – Abraham als den Gründer des »antiken« rituellen Kultus und Muḥammad als den Voll-
ender des »spätantiken« verbalen Kultus – zu einer

practice. As much as the community in Medina established itself upon the figure of Abraham, and ultimately understood itself as an Abrahamic faith, a *millat Ibrāhīm*, Islam, which was born in the epistemic space of late antiquity, did not emerge as a religion based on sacrifice, but as a religion based on the word, on the Quranic discourse with and about God. This development semantically rests upon biblical and ancient Arabic traditions, but it became possible only through the use of different registers of typology, through the special intertextual thinking which underlies the hermeneutics of late antiquity.

neuen, liturgischen Synergie zusammenführt. Der im Denkraum der Spätantike geborene Islam ist eben – so sehr sich die Gemeinde auch bei ihrer Identitätssuche in Medina an der Figur Abrahams aufrichtete und sich schließlich selbst als abrahamitische Glaubensrichtung, als *millat Ibrāhīm* verstand – doch keine auf dem Opfer, sondern eine auf dem Wort, der koranischen Gottesrede, basierende Religion. Diese Entwicklung ruht semantisch auf biblischen und altarabischen Traditionen, sie wurde aber erst möglich durch den Einsatz verschiedener Register von Typologie, durch das besondere intertextuelle Denken, das der Hermeneutik der Spätantike zugrunde liegt.

Notes

1 See Christoph Schulte, »Kritik und ›Aufhebung‹ der jüdischen Literatur in der frühen Wissenschaft des Judentums,« in »*Im vollen Licht der Geschichte*« – *Die Wissenschaft des Judentums und die Anfänge der kritischen Koranforschung*, eds. Dirk Hartwig, et al. (Würzburg: Ergon-Verlag, 2008), 99–109.

2 See Friedrich Niewöhner, »Von Muhammad zu Jesus: Abraham Geigers Schrift über den Koran,« in Abraham Geiger, *Was hat Mohammed aus dem Judenthume aufgenommen?* (Berlin: Parerga, 2005), 7–33.

3 Cited in Christoph Schulte, »Kritik und ›Aufhebung,‹« 101.

4 See Gershom Scholem, »Wissenschaft vom Judentum einst und jetzt,« in idem, *Judaica I*, ed. Rolf Tiedemann (Frankfurt: Suhrkamp, 1963), 147–164.

5 See Maurice Olender, *Les Langues du Paradis*: *Aryans et Sémites, un couple providentiel* (Paris: Gallimard, 1989).

6 Friedrich Niewöhner, »Von Muhammad zu Jesus,« 7–33.

7 Thomas Rahe, »Leopold Zunz und die Wissenschaft des Judentums,« in *Judaica: Beiträge zum Verstehen des Judentums* 42/3 (1986), 188–199.

8 See David Niremberg, *Wie jüdisch war das Spanien des Mittelalters? Die Perspektive der Literatur* (Trier: Kliomedia, 2005).

9 Moritz Steinschneider, *Die arabische Literatur der Juden* (Frankfurt: Kauffmann, 1902).

10 Ute Franke, et al., eds., *Roads of Arabia*: *Archaeological Treasures of Saudi Arabia* (Berlin: Wasmuth, 2011).

11 Angelika Neuwirth, *Der Koran als Text der Spätantike*: *Ein europäischer Zugang* (Berlin: Verlag der Weltreligionen, 2010).

12 For Horovitz, see Gudrun Jäger, »Josef Horovitz,« in »*Im vollen Licht der Geschichte*,« ed. Hartwig, 117–130.

13 For Speyer, see Franz Rosenthal, »Heinrich Speyer,« in »*Im vollen Licht der Geschichte*,« ed. Hartwig, 113–116.

14 Felix Körner, unpublished dossier.

15 Guy Stroumsa, *Das Ende des Opferkults*: *Die religiösen Mutationen der Spätantike* (Berlin: Verlag der Weltreligionen, 2011).

16 Rudolf Sellheim, »Prophet, Caliph und Geschichte: Die Muhammad-Biographie des Ibn Ishaq,« in *Oriens* 18–19 (1967), 33–91.

Anmerkungen

1 Siehe Christoph Schulte, Kritik und ›Aufhebung‹ der jüdischen Literatur in der frühen Wissenschaft des Judentums, in: Dirk Hartwig [u.a.] (Hgg.), »Im vollen Licht der Geschichte« – Die Wissenschaft des Judentums und die Anfänge der kritischen Koranforschung, Würzburg 2008, 99–109.

2 Siehe Friedrich Niewöhner, Von Muhammad zu Jesus. Abraham Geigers Schrift über den Koran, in: Abraham Geiger, Was hat Mohammed aus dem Judenthume aufgenommen? Berlin 2005, 7–33.

3 Zitiert nach Schulte, Kritik (wie Anm. 1), 101.

4 Siehe Gershom Scholem, Wissenschaft vom Judentum einst und jetzt, in: Gershom Scholem, Judaica I, Frankfurt 1963, 147–164.

5 Siehe Maurice Olender, Les Langues du Paradis: Aryans et Sémites, un couple providential, Paris 1989.

6 Niewöhner, Muhammad (wie Anm. 2), 7–33.

7 Thomas Rahe, Leopold Zunz und die Wissenschaft des Judentums, in: Judaica 42/3 (1986), 188–199.

8 Siehe David Niremberg, Wie jüdisch war das Spanien des Mittelalters? Die Perspektive der Literatur. Trier 2005.

9 Moritz Steinschneider, Die arabische Literatur der Juden, Frankfurt (Main) 1902.

10 Ute Franke [u.a.] (Hgg)., Roads of Arabia: Archaeological Treasures of Saudi Arabia, Berlin 2011.

11 Angelika Neuwirth, Der Koran als Text der Spätantike. Ein europäischer Zugang, Berlin 2010.

12 Zu Horovitz siehe Gudrun Jäger, Josef Horovitz, in: Hartwig, Licht (wie Anm. 1), 117–130.

13 Zu Speyer siehe Franz Rosenthal, Heinrich Speyer, in: Hartwig, Licht (wie Anm. 1), 113–116.

14 Felix Körner, unveröffentlichtes Dossier.

15 Guy Stroumsa, Das Ende des Opferkults. Die religiösen Mutationen der Spätantike, 2. Aufl. Berlin 2012.

16 Rudolf Sellheim, Prophet, Caliph und Geschichte: Die Muhammad-Biographie des Ibn Ishaq, in: Oriens 18/19 (1967), 33–91.

17 Siehe dazu Georges Vajda, [Art.] Isrāʾīliyyāt, in: Encyclopaedia of Islam 4 (2nd ed.), Leiden 1973, 211–212.

17 See Georges Vajda, »Isrā'īliyyāt,« in *Encyclopaedia of Islam*, vol. 4, 2nd ed. (Leiden: Brill, 1973), 211–212.

18 Sidney Griffith, *The Bible in Arabic: The Scripture of the People of the Book in Arabic Language* (Princeton, N.J.: Princeton University Press, 2013).

19 The most telling example may be the »Babel-Bibel Streit,« see Reinhard G. Lehmann, *Friedrich Delitzsch und der Babel-Bibel-Streit* (*Orbis Biblicus et Orientalis*, vol. 133) (Göttingen: Vandenhoeck und Ruprecht, 1994).

20 One might think of *The book of the religious communities and sects* by Muḥammad al-Shahrastānī (died 1153).

21 To Burḥanaddīn al-Biqāʿī (died 1480), who studied the bible intensively, see Walid Saleh, *In Defense of the Bible: A Critical Edition and an Introduction to al-Biqāʿī's Bible Treatise* (Leiden: Brill, 2008).

22 For the intensified Jewish-Islamic exchange at this time, see Hava Lazarus-Yafeh, *Intertwined Worlds: Medieval Islam and Bible Criticism* (Princeton, N.J.: Princeton University Press, 1992), 127–128.

23 For ʿAbduh, see Rotraud Wielandt, *Offenbarung und Geschichte im Denken moderner Muslime* (Wiesbaden: Franz Steiner Verlag, 1971), 49–72.

24 For Riḍā, see Wielandt, *Offenbarung und Geschichte*, 73–94.

25 Thomas Bauer, *Die Kultur der Ambiguität: Eine andere Geschichte des Islams* (Berlin: Verlag der Weltreligionen, 2013).

26 Peter Heath, »Creative Hermeneutics: A Comparative Analysis of Three Islamic Approaches,« in *Arabica* 36 (1989), 173–210.

27 See Katajun Amirpur, *Den Islam neu denken: Der Dschihad für Demokratie, Freiheit und Frauenrechte* (München: Beck, 2013).

28 For Horovitz, see Gudrun Jäger, »Josef Horovitz,« in *»Im vollen Licht der Geschichte«*, ed. Hartwig, 117–130.

29 See especially Gotthelf Bergsträsser, »Koranlesung in Kairo« (with a contribution by Karl Huber), in *Der Islam* 20 (1932), 1–42; and in *Der Islam* 21 (1932), 110–140.

30 Johann Fück, »Die Originalität des arabischen Propheten,« in *Zeitschrift der Deutschen Morgenländischen Gesellschaft* 90 (1936), 509–525; Montgomery Watt, *Muhammad at Mecca* (Oxford: Clarendon Press, 1953); idem, *Muhammad at Medina* (Oxford: Clarendon Press, 1956).

18 Sidney Griffith, The Bible in Arabic. The Scripture of the People of the Book in Arabic Language, Princeton 2013.

19 Das sprechendste Beispiel dürfte der Babel-Bibel-Streit sein, siehe Reinhard G. Lehmann, Friedrich Delitzsch und der Babel-Bibel-Streit (Orbis Biblicus et Orientalis 133), Göttingen 1994.

20 Man denke an »Das Buch der Religionsgemeinschaften und der Sekten« von Muḥammad al-Shahrastānī (gest. 1153).

21 Zu Burhānaddīn al-Biqāʾī (gest. 1480), der intensive Bibelstudien betrieb, siehe Walid Saleh, In Defense of the Bible. A critical edition and an Introduction to al-Biqīʾs Bible Treatise, Edinburgh 2006.

22 Siehe zu dem intensivierten jüdisch-islamischen Austausch in dieser Zeit Hava Lazarus-Yafeh, Intertwined Worlds. Medieval Islam and Bible Criticism, Princeton 1992, 127–128.

23 Zu ʿAbduh siehe Rotraud Wielandt, Offenbarung und Geschichte im Denken moderner Muslime, Wiesbaden 1971, 49–72.

24 Zu Riḍā siehe Wielandt, a. a. O., 73–94.

25 Thomas Bauer, Die Kultur der Ambiguität. Eine andere Geschichte des Islams, Berlin 2013.

26 Peter Heath, Creative Hermeneutics: A Comparative Analysis of Three Islamic Approaches, in: Arabica 36 (1989), 173–210.

27 Siehe dazu Katajun Amirpur, Den Islam neu denken. Der Dschihad für Demokratie, Freiheit und Frauenrechte, München 2013.

28 Siehe zu Horovitz Gudrun Jäger, Josef Horovitz, in: Hartwig, Licht (wie Anm. 1), 117–130.

29 Siehe insbesondere Gotthelf Bergsträsser, Koranlesung in Kairo (mit einem Beitrag von Karl Huber), in: Der Islam 20 (1932), 1–42; 21 (1932), 110–140.

30 Johann Fück, Die Originalität des arabischen Propheten, in: Zeitschrift der Deutschen Morgenländischen Gesellschaft 90 (1936), 509–525; Montgomery Watt, Muhammad at Mecca, Edinburgh 1953; Montgomery Watt, Muhammad at Medina, Edinburgh 1956.

31 John Wansbrough, Quranic Studies: Sources and Methods of Scriptural Interpretation, Oxford 1977.

32 Patricia Crone/Michael Cook, Hagarism: The Making of the Islamic World, Cambridge 1977.

31 John Wansbrough, *Quranic Studies: Sources and Methods of Scriptural Interpretation* (Oxford: Oxford University Press, 1977).

32 Patricia Crone and Michael Cook, *Hagarism: The Making of the Islamic World* (Cambridge: Cambridge University Press, 1977).

33 Michael Marx, »Ein Koranforschungsprojekt in der Tradition der Wissenschaft des Judentums: Zur Programmatik des Akademienvorhabens Corpus Coranicum,« in »*Im vollen Licht der Geschichte*«, ed. Hartwig, 41–54.

34 Thomas Bauer, *Die Kultur der Ambiguität.*

35 Mohammed Arkoun, *The Unthought in Contemporary Islamic Thought* (London: Saqi Books, 2002).

36 For Nasr Hmid Abu Zaid, see Navid Kermani, *Offenbarung als Kommunikation: Das Konzept waḥy in Naṣr Ḥāmid Abū Zayd's 'Mafhūm al-naṣṣ'* (Frankfurt: Lang, 1996); to Shabestari and Sorush, see Katajun Amirpur, *Islam neu denken.*

37 Jane Dammen McAuliffe, ed., *The Encyclopedia of the Qur'an*, 6 vols. (Leiden: Brill, 2000–2006).

38 See, for example, Susanne Heine, Ömer Özsoy, Christoph Schwöbel and Abdullah Takim, eds., *Christen und Muslime im Gespräch: Eine Verständigung über Kernthemen der Theologie* (Gütersloh: Gütersloher Verlagshaus, 2014); and, especially, Karl-Josef Kuschel, *Juden, Christen, Muslime: Herkunft und Zukunft* (Ostfildern: Patmos, 2007).

39 This is addressed extensively in Nora Schmidt, Nora Katharina Schmid, Angelika Neuwirth, eds., *Denkraum Spätantike. Reflexionen von Antiken im Umfeld des Koran* (Wiesbaden: Harrassowitz, 2016).

40 Aziz al-Azmeh, *The Emergence of Islam in Late Antiquity* (Cambridge: Cambridge University Press, 2014), xi.

41 Peter Brown, *The World of Late Antiquity: AD 150–750* (London: Thames & Hudson, 2002), 191.

42 Samir Kassir, *Being Arab* [*Considérations sur le malheur arabe*, 2004], transl. Will Hobson (London: Verso, 2013), 33.

43 See the introduction in Nora Schmidt, et al., eds. *Denkraum Spätantike* (like note 39).

44 Angelika Neuwirth, *Scripture, Poetry and the Making of a Community: Reading the Qur'an as a Literary Text* (Oxford: Oxford University Press, 2014), 53–75.

33 Michael Marx, Ein Koranforschungsprojekt in der Tradition der Wissenschaft des Judentums: Zur Programmatik des Akademienvorhabens Corpus Coranicum, in: Hartwig. Licht (wie Anm. 1), 41–54.

34 Thomas Bauer, Die Kultur der Ambiguität. Eine andere Geschichte des Islam, Berlin 2011.

35 Mohammed Arkoun, The Unthought in Contemporary Islamic Thought, London 2002.

36 Siehe zu Nasr Hmid Abu Zaid Navid Kermani, Offenbarung als Kommunikation: Das Konzept *waḥy in Naṣr Ḥāmid Abū Zayd's* ›*Mafhūm al-naṣṣ*‹, Frankfurt (Main) 1996; siehe zu Shabestari und Sorush Katajun Amirpur, Islam (wie Anm. 27).

37 Jane Dammen McAuliffe (Hg.), The Encyclopedia of the Qur'an, 6 Bde, Leiden 2000–2006.

38 Siehe etwa Susanne Heine [u.a.] (Hgg.), Christen und Muslime im Gespräch. Eine Verständigung über Kernthemen der Theologie, Gütersloh 2014; siehe insbesondere aber Karl-Josef Kuschel, Juden, Christen, Muslime. Herkunft und Zukunft, Ostfildern 2007.

39 Er wird ausführlich begründet in Nora Schmidt/Nora Katharina Schmid/Angelika Neuwirth (Hgg.): Denkraum Spätantike. Reflexionen von Antiken im Umfeld des Koran. Wiesbaden 2016.

40 Aziz al-Azmeh, The Emergence of Islam in Late Antiquity, London (2014), XI.

41 Peter Brown, The World of Late Antiquity: AD 150–750, London 2002.

42 Samir Kassir, Das arabische Unglück, Berlin 2006.

43 Siehe dazu die Einleitung zu Nora Schmidt [u.a.] (Hgg.), Denkraum Spätantike (wie Anm. 39).

44 Angelika Neuwirth, Scripture, Poetry and the Making of a Community. Reading the Qur'an as a Literary Text, Oxford 2014, 53–75.

45 Andras Hamori, On the Art of Medieval Arabic Literature, Princeton 1974.

46 Jan Assmann, Das kulturelle Gedächtnis: Schrift, Erinnerung und politische Identität in frühen Hochkulturen, Munich 1992.

45 Andras Hamori, *On the Art of Medieval Arabic Literature* (Princeton, N.J.: Princeton University Press, 1974).

46 Jan Assmann, *Das kulturelle Gedächtnis: Schrift, Erinnerung und politische Identität in frühen Hochkulturen* (Munich: Beck, 1992).

47 Angelika Neuwirth, »The ›Discovery of Writing‹ in the Qur'an: Tracing an Epistemic Revolution in Late Antiquity«, in *Qur'an and Adab. The Shaping of Literary Traditions in Classical Islam*, ed. Nuha Alshaar (Oxford: Oxford University Press in association with the Institute of Ismaili Studies, 2017), 61–92.

48 Ute Franke, et al., eds., *Roads of Arabia: Archaeological Treasures of Saudi Arabia* (Berlin: Wasmuth, 2011).

49 James Montgomery, »The Empty Ḥijāz,« in *Arabic Theology, Arabic Philosophy: From the Many to the One*, ed. idem (Leuven: Peeters, 2006), 37–97.

50 Theodor Nöldeke, Friedrich Schwally, Gotthelf Bergsträsser and Otto Pretzl, *Die Geschichte des Korantextes* (Leipzig: Dieterich, 1938).

51 Regarding this style of commentary and its most important representative, Alī ibn Aḥmad al-Wāḥidī (death 1075), see Andrew Rippin, *The Qur'ān and its interpretative tradition* (Aldershot: Ashgate, 2001).

52 Angelika Neuwirth, »Jesus und Muhammad – zwei spätantike Lehrer? Ein Versuch, den Koran im Licht der Lehre Jesu neu zu lesen,« in *Jesus Christus: Von alttestamentlichen Messiasvorstellungen bis zur literarischen Figur*, ed. Thomas Fornet-Ponse (Münster: Aschendorff, 2015), 133–148.

53 According to the classical definition given by Henning Graf Reventlow, *Epochen der Bibelauslegung*, vol. 1, *Vom Alten Testament bis Origines* (München: Beck, 1990), 66, typology is »a juxtaposition of events and persons of an older narrative with those of a later period, whereby the latter stands in opposition to the earlier or fulfills and overcomes it.« For a classification of the Quranic typologies, see Zishan Ghaffar, »Jesus redivivus: Der koranische Jesus im Kontext von Prophetologie«, in *Jesus Christus*, ed. Fornet-Ponse, 149–162.

54 Suzanne Pinckney Stetkevych, *The Mute Immortals Speak: Pre-Islamic Poetry and the Poetics of Rituals* (Ithaca, N.Y.: Cornell University Press, 1993).

47 Angelika Neuwirth, The »Discovery of Writing« in the Qur'an: Tracing an Epistemic Revolution in Late Antiquity, in: Nuha Alshaar (Hg.), Qur'an and Adab. The Shaping of Literary Traditions in Classical Islam. Oxford: Oxford University Press in association with the Institute of Ismaili Studies 2017, 61–92.

48 Franke, Roads (wie Anm. 10).

49 James Montgomery, The Empty Ḥijāz, in: James Montgomery (Hg.), Arabic Theology, Arabic Philosophy, From the Many to the One. Leuven 2006, 37–97.

50 Theodor Nöldeke [u.a.], Die Geschichte des Korantextes, Leipzig 1938.

51 Zu dieser Kommentargattung und ihrem wichtigsten Vertreter Alī ibn Aḥmad al-Wāḥidī (gest. 1075) siehe Andrew Rippin, The Qur'ān and its interpretative tradition, London 2002.

52 Angelika Neuwirth, Jesus und Muhammad – zwei spätantike Lehrer? Ein Versuch, den Koran im Licht der Lehre Jesu neu zu lesen, in: Thomas Fornet-Ponse (Hg.), Jesus Christus. Von alttestamentlichen Messiasvorstellungen bis zur literarischen Figur, Münster 2015, 133–148.

53 Nach der klassischen Definition von Henning Graf Reventlow, Epochen der Bibelauslegung, Bd. 1, Vom Alten Testament bis Origines, München 1990, 66, ist Typologie »eine Gegenüberstellung von Ereignissen und Personen der früheren Geschichte zu denen aus einer späteren Periode, wobei das Spätere zum Früheren entweder im Gegensatz steht oder eine Überhöhung bildet«. Für eine Klassifikation koranischer Typologien siehe Zishan Ghaffar, Jesus redivivus. Der koranische Jesus im Kontext von Prophetologie, in: Fornet-Ponse, Jesus Christus (wie Anm. 52), 149–162.

54 Suzanne Pinckney Stetkevych, The Mute Immortals Speak. Pre-Islamic Poetry and the Poetics of Rituals. Ithaca 1993.

55 Angelika Neuwirth, Der Koran I. Frühmekkanische Suren, Poetische Prophetie, Berlin 2011.

56 Georges Tamer, Zeit und Gott: Hellenistische Zeitvorstellungen in der altarabischen Dichtung und im Koran, Berlin 2008.

57 Angelika Neuwirth, *Qur'ānic* Readings of the Psalms, in: Angelika Neuwirth [u.a.] (Hgg.), The *Qur'ān* in Context, *Historical and Literary Investigations into the Qur'anic Milieu*, Leiden 2011, 733–778.

55 Angelika Neuwirth, *Der Koran I. Frühmekkanische Suren*, Poetische Prophetie (Berlin: Verlag der Weltreligionen, 2011).

56 Georges Tamer, *Zeit und Gott: Hellenistische Zeitvorstellungen in der altarabischen Dichtung und im Koran* (Berlin: de Gruyter, 2008).

57 Angelika Neuwirth, »Qur'ānic Readings of the Psalms,« in *The Qur'ān in Context: Historical and Literary Investigations into the Qur'anic Milieu*, eds. Angelika Neuwirth, Nicolai Sinai and Michael Marx (Leiden: Brill, 2011), 733–778. The English translation of the Quran cited above and below is *The Qur'an*, transl. M. A. S. Abdel Haleem (Oxford: Oxford University Press, 2005).

58 Angelika Neuwirth, »The Spiritual Meaning of Jerusalem in Islam,« in *City of the Great King: Jerusalem from David to the Present*, ed. Nitza Rosovsky (Cambridge, Mass.: Harvard University Press, 1996), 93–116 and 483–495.

59 See James Kugel, *How to Read the Bible: A Guide to Scripture, Then and Now* (New York, N.Y.: Free Press, 2007), 9–17.

60 For manifestations of prophecy continuing on the Arabian Peninsula, see Christian Robin, »Les Signes de la prophétie en Arabie a l'époque de Mohammad (fin de VIᵉ et début du VIIᵉ siècle de l'ère chrétienne),« in *La Raison des signes: Présages, rites, destin dans les sociétés de la Méditerranée ancienne*, eds. Stella Georgoudi, Renée Koch Piettre and Francis Schmidt (Leiden: Brill, 2012), here 433–475.

61 Cf. Neuwirth, *Der Koran als Text der Spätantike*, 24–31.

62 Neuwirth, *Der Koran als Text der Spätantike*, 711–716.

63 It is narrated in Q 37:83–98, 26:69–86, 19:41–50, 43:26–7, 21:51–73, 29:16–27, 6:74–84, 60:4; see Heinrich Speyer, *Die biblischen Erzählungen in Qoran* (Hildesheim: Olms, 1988), 130–140.

64 Cf. Nicolai Sinai, *Fortschreibung und Auslegung: Studien zur frühen Koraninterpretation* (Wiesbaden: Harrassowitz Verlag, 2009), 117, and Neuwirth, *Der Koran als Text der Spätantike*, 633–652.

65 Cf. Neuwirth, *Der Koran als Text der Spätantike*, 451–509.

66 The two later appended verses 112–113 are already a part of the polemical debate that was held in Medina regarding the merits of the fathers; they are only associatively related to the narrative.

67 See Rudi Paret, *Der Koran: Kommentar und Konkordanz* (Stuttgart/Berlin/Köln: Kohlhammer 1993), 417.

58 Angelika Neuwirth, The Spiritual Meaning of Jerusalem in Islam, in: Nitza Rosovsky (Hg.), City of the Great King. Jerusalem from Daxid to the present, Cambridge 1996, 93–116 und 483–495.

59 Siehe dazu James Kugel, How to Read the Bible. A Guide to Scripture, Then and Now, New York 2007, 9–17.

60 Zu der Sondererscheinung der noch fortwirkenden Prophetie auf der arabischen Halbinsel siehe Christian Robin, Les Signes de la prophétie en Arabie a l'époche de Mohammad (fin de VIe et début du VIIe siècle de l'ère chrétienne), in: Stella Georgoudi/Renée Koch Piettre/Francis Schmidt (Hgg.), La Raison des signes. Présages, rites, destin dans les sociétés de la Méditerranée ancienne, Leiden 2012, hier 433–475.

61 Vgl. Neuwirth, Koran (wie Anm. 11), 24–31.

62 A. a. O., 711–716.

63 Sie wird erzählt in Q 37:83–98, 26:69–86, 19:41–50, 43:26–27, 21:51–73, 29:16–27, 6:74–84, 60:4; s. Heinrich Speyer, Die biblischen Erzählungen im Qoran, Gräfenhainichen 1931, 130–140.

64 Vgl. Nicolai Sinai, Fortschreibung und Auslegung. Studien zur frühen Koraninterpretation, Wiesbaden 2009, 117, und Neuwirth, Koran (wie Anm. 11), 633–652.

65 Vgl. a. a. O., 451–509.

66 Die beiden später angefügten Verse 112–113 sind bereits Teil der in Medina ausgetragenen polemischen Auseinandersetzung über die Verdienste der Väter; sie haben mit der Erzählung nur assoziativ zu tun.

67 Siehe Rudi Paret, Der Koran, Kommentar und Konkordanz, Stuttgart/Berlin/Köln 1993, 417.

68 Vgl. James L. Kugel, The Bible as it Was, 4. print, Cambridge, Mass. 2000, 177.

69 Angelika Neuwirth/Karl Neuwirth, Sūrat al-Fātiḥa: »Eröffnung« des Text-Corpus Koran oder »Introitus« der Gebetsliturgie?, in: Walter Gross (Hg.), Text, Methode und Grammatik. Wolfgang Richter zum 65. Geburtstag, St. Ottilien 1991, 331–357.

70 Siehe dazu Neuwirth, Koran (wie Anm. 11), 321–327.

71 Sinai, Fortschreibung (wie Anm. 64), 134.

72 Ebd.

73 Vgl. Neuwirth, Koran (wie Anm. 11), 510–560.

68 Cf. James L. Kugel, *The Bible as it was* (Cambridge, Mass.: Belknap Press of Harvard University Press, 1997), 177.

69 Angelika Neuwirth and Karl Neuwirth, »Sūrat al-Fātiḥa: ›Eröffnung‹ des Text-Corpus Koran oder ›Introitus‹ der Gebetsliturgie?« in *Text, Methode und Grammatik: Wolfgang Richter zum 65. Geburtstag*, ed. Walter Gross (St. Ottilien: EOS-Verlag, 1991), 331–357.

70 See Neuwirth, *Der Koran als Text der Spätantike*, 321–127.

71 Nicolai Sinai, *Fortschreibung und Auslegung*, 134.

72 Ibid.

73 Cf. Neuwirth, *Der Koran als Text der Spätantike*, 510–560.

74 To the conception of the substitutionary sacrifice which was established with the Akedah, see Adin Steinsaltz, *The Essential Talmud* (London: Weidenfeld and Nicolson, 1976), 176.

75 Snouck Hurgronje, »The Meccan Feast (Het Mekaanse Feest),« in *The Development of Islamic Ritual*, ed. Gerald Hawting (Aldershot: Ashgate, 2006), 239–269.

76 With regard to the Quran itself, there is little more information about the Islamic *ḥajj* (which is taking shape here) than that which is found in the suras 2:158, 189–203, 3:94–97, 9:3, 19 and 22:27–29; yet it is to be presumed with Julius Wellhausen and Gerald Hawting (»Pilgrimage« in EQ III. 2003, 98) that the already practiced Hajj was a ritual act with various parts that culminated in a sacrifice.

77 Ibid.

78 Tilman Seidensticker, »Quellen zur vorislamischen Religionsgeschichte,« in *Asiatische Studien* 57 (2003), 881–892.

79 Sinai, *Fortschreibung und Auslegung*, 130.

80 Hurgronje, »The Meccan Feast.«

81 Julius Wellhausen, *Reste arabischen Heidentums*, 3rd ed. (Berlin: de Gruyter, 1961), here (to the Hajj) 79–94.

82 Joseph Witztum, »The Foundation of the House (Q 2:127),« in *Bulletin of the School of Oriental and African Studies* 72 (2009), 25–40.

83 Cf. Kugel, *The Bible as it was*, 175.

84 Sinai, *Fortschreibung und Auslegung*, 141 f.

85 Ibid., 142.

74 S. zu der mit der Akedah gestifteten Vorstellung des stellvertretenden Opfers Adin Steinsaltz, The Essential Talmud, New York 1976, 176.

75 Snouck Hurgronje, The Meccan Feast (Het Mekaanse Feest), in: Gerald Hawting (Hg.), The Development of Islamic Ritual, Aldershot 2006, 239–269.

76 Aus dem Koran selbst lässt sich wenig mehr über den nun Gestalt annehmenden islamischen *ḥadjdj* entnehmen als die Suren 2:158,189–203, 3:94–97, 9:3,19 und 22:27–29 enthalten, doch ist mit Julius Wellhausen und Gerald Hawting, »Pilgrimage« in EQ III, 2003, 98) davon auszugehen, dass bereits der vorgefundene *ḥadjdj* eine aus verschiedenen Riten bestehende Kulthandlung war, die im Opfer kulminierte.

77 Ebd.

78 Tilman Seidensticker, Quellen zur vorislamischen Religionsgeschichte, in: Asiatische Studien 57 (2003), 881–892.

79 Sinai, Fortschreibung (wie Anm. 64), 130.

80 Hurgronje, Feast (wie Anm. 75).

81 Julius Wellhausen, Reste arabischen Heidentums, Berlin 1961, hier (zum *ḥadjdj*) 79–94.

82 Joseph Witztum, The Foundation of the House (Q 2:127), in: Bulletin of the School of Oriental and African Studies 72 (2009), 25–40.

83 Vgl. Kugel, Bible (wie Anm. 68), 175.

84 Sinai, Fortschreibung (wie Anm. 64), 141 f.

85 A. a. O., 142.

86 Deswegen wird auch die Figur Ismaels weder im Koran noch im Islam theologisch nachhaltig wirksam. Bis heute wird in der Tradition, die den Koran nicht diachron liest, sondern Vers-für-Vers interpretiert, die Frage, wer zum Opfer ausersehen war, kontrovers diskutiert. Sie erscheint aber weniger wichtig. Das Verdienst liegt in Gänze bei Abraham. Ismael ist in der Tradition zwar Stammvater der Araber, er überträgt aber keine Autorität auf seine Nachkommen.

86 For this reason, the figure of Ishmael does not become theologically significant in the Quran or in Islam in a lasting way. To this day, the question is discussed controversially in the tradition (which does not read the Quran diachronically, but rather interprets it verse-by-verse) regarding who the designated victim was. This appears to be little important, however; the merit lies entirely with Abraham. In tradition, Ishmael is indeed the progenitor of the Arabs, but he transfers no authority to his descendants.

Address
at the Award Ceremony of the
2015 Dr. Leopold Lucas Prize

by

Jürgen Kampmann

Ansprache
bei der Verleihung des
Dr. Leopold Lucas-Preises 2015

von

Jürgen Kampmann

Dear Honorary Senator Dr. Lucas, Guests, Representatives of the Administration of our University, Prorector Assmann and Chancellor Rothfuß, Deans of Faculties, Colleagues, Ladies and Gentlemen – and in particular, Prof. Dr. Dr. h.c. Neuwirth and Dr. Heinemeyer!

On behalf of Eberhard-Karls-University as a whole and the Protestant Faculty of Theology in particular, I have the pleasant task of welcoming you here today! The purpose of this ceremony is to award the Dr. Leopold Lucas Prize and the Dr. Leopold Lucas Junior Scholar Prize for 2015. We do not have only two tasks today, however, but three:

– We are excited about what the prize winner, Professor Dr. Angelika Neuwirth, will share in her lecture today, which is titled »How does Scripture Emerge? The Hebrew Bible and the Quran.«

Sehr verehrter, lieber Herr Ehrensenator Dr. Lucas, sehr verehrte, geladene Gäste, verehrte Repräsentanten der Leitung unserer Universität, Herr Prorektor Assmann und Herr Kanzler Rothfuß, Spectabiles, liebe Kolleginnen und Kollegen, ganz besonders aber: sehr verehrte Preisträger des heutigen Tages, Frau Kollegin Professor Dr. Dr. h.c. Neuwirth und Herr Dr. Heinemeyer!

Mir kommt die angenehme Aufgabe zu, Sie hier im Namen der Eberhard-Karls-Universität insgesamt und der Evangelisch-Theologischen Fakultät insbesondere willkommen zu heißen! Die heutige Feierstunde dient der Verleihung des Dr. Leopold Lucas-Preises sowie des Dr. Leopold Lucas-Nachwuchswissenschaftlerpreises für das Jahr 2015. Wir gehen damit aber jetzt nicht nur auf zwei, sondern auf drei Aufgaben zu:

– Gespannt sind wir auf das, was uns die Preisträgerin, Frau Professor Dr. Angelika Neuwirth, in ihrem Vortrag unter dem Titel »Wie entsteht eine Schrift? Die hebräische Bibel und der Koran« vermitteln wird.

– Of course, we shall also have a closer look at the academic work of both the prize winner and the winner of the Junior Scholar Prize.

– Not least, however, but rather first and foremost, the concern that stands behind the awarding of these prizes is to be remembered. This is to be called to memory in such a way that the work and desire of Dr. Leopold Lucas – to whose memory these prizes are awarded – are encountered not only as a historical reminiscence but also as something tackling us today, here and now.

We shall begin with this latter task. That which characterized the life of Dr. Leopold Lucas may already be known to many in outline. Indeed, many may be familiar with it, especially those who have paid attention to this in the award ceremonies over the years. Nevertheless, this information which marks the life of Leopold Lucas shall again be called to memory here. Even in the age of a modularized and hasty course of study with the continuous gathering and adding up of credit points on module certificates and in the »Transcripts of Records«, the old principle *Repetitio est mater studiorum* has lost nothing of its beneficial effect, one which impresses the issues upon us, if it is heeded.

Leopold Lucas was born in 1872 in Marburg an der Lahn. There he passed in 1892 the *Abitur* and then

– Natürlich soll auch ein Einblick gegeben werden in das wissenschaftliche Werk der Preisträgerin sowie in die Arbeit des Preisträgers des Nachwuchswissenschaftlerpreises, und

– ganz und gar nicht zuletzt, sondern zu allererst soll das Anliegen, das hinter dieser Preisverleihung steht, in Erinnerung gerufen werden – in einer Weise, dass uns das Wirken und Wollen von Dr. Leopold Lucas, zu dessen Gedächtnis diese Preise ja verliehen werden, nicht nur als eine historische Reminiszenz begegnet, sondern uns auch hier und jetzt anmutet.

Beginnen wir mit dieser letztgenannten Aufgabe. Das, was den Lebensweg von Dr. Leopold Lucas geprägt hat, dürfte vielen, die den Preisverleihungen schon in früheren Jahren ihre Aufmerksamkeit geschenkt und ihnen beigewohnt haben, in Umrissen schon bekannt, ja vertraut sein. Dennoch sei hier noch einmal an die äußeren Daten erinnert, die den Lebensweg von Leopold Lucas markieren – auch im Zeitalter eines modularisierten, eiligen Studienbetriebs und des dazu gehörigen kontinuierlichen Sammelns und Aufaddierens von Leistungspunkten auf Modulscheinen und in »Transcripts of Records« hat der alte Grundsatz »Repetitio est mater studiorum« nichts von seiner heilsamen, die Sachverhalte einprägenden Wirkung eingebüßt, wenn er denn beherzigt wird.

Leopold Lucas hat das Licht der Welt 1872 in Marburg an der Lahn erblickt. Dort legte er 1892 das

went on to study oriental languages, history, philosophy and Jewish studies at university in Berlin and
also simultaneously at the College for Jewish Studies.
On the 19th of December, 1895, he received his Doc-
tor of Philosophy degree in Tübingen. He wrote his
dissertation on the history of the city of Tyre at the
time of the Crusades and his doctoral adviser was the
historian Bernhard von Kugler.[1] Leopold Lucas's academic interest was especially dedicated to the history
of the high middle ages and also the fourth century,
as his book *The History of Jews in the Fourth Century*
(1910) shows.[2] Professionally, he served the Jewish
congregation in Glogau in Lower Silesia for many
years (from 1899 onwards) as a rabbi. He did this until
he was called to Berlin to lecture at the Educational
Institution (College) for Jewish Studies, in the subject
area of Biblical literature and history (especially the
history of the early middle ages). Together with his
wife, Dora Janower, whom he married in 1904, he
became a victim of the National Socialist racial ideology. He died in the Theresienstadt concentration
camp on the 10th of September, 1943.[3]

It is immediately recognizable and requires no
lengthy justification that the question regarding the
academic work of the person, to whose memory this
prize was established, should stand in the foreground
at the awarding of a prize and a junior scholar prize

Abitur ab und studierte danach an der Universität in Berlin wie auch zugleich an der Hochschule für die Wissenschaft des Judentums orientalische Sprachen, Geschichte, Philosophie und Wissenschaften des Judentums. Am 19. Dezember 1895 ist er dann hier in Tübingen zum Dr. phil. promoviert worden – er hatte bei dem Historiker Bernhard von Kugler eine Dissertation zur Geschichte der Stadt Tyrus zur Zeit der Kreuzzüge vorgelegt.[1] Leopold Lucas' wissenschaftliches Interesse galt in besonderer Weise der Geschichte in der Epoche des Hochmittelalters, aber auch der des 4. Jahrhunderts; sein 1910 erschienenes Werk »Zur Geschichte der Juden im vierten Jahrhundert« dokumentiert das.[2] Beruflich hat er der jüdischen Gemeinde in Glogau in Niederschlesien über viele Jahre – von 1899 an – als Rabbiner gedient, bis er nach Berlin berufen wurde an die Lehranstalt (Hochschule) für die Wissenschaft des Judentums, um dort als Dozent für biblische Literatur und Geschichte (besonders der Geschichte des frühen Mittelalters) zu wirken. Mit seiner Ehefrau Dora Janower, mit er 1904 die Ehe schloss, wurde dann auch er ein Opfer der nationalsozialistischen Rassenideologie – im Konzentrationslager Theresienstadt ließ er am 10. September 1943 sein Leben.[3]

Dass nun bei der Verleihung eines Preises sowie eines Nachwuchswissenschaftlerpreises durch eine Universität die Frage nach dem wissenschaftlichen Werk desjenigen, zu dessen Gedächtnis der Preis gestiftet ist, im Vordergrund steht, ist sofort und ohne

by a university. The academic work of Leopold Lucas has already been addressed in various regards at the award ceremonies over the past years. Lucas's publications are characterized by very precise historical work. Whoever has had a look at his dissertation, »The History of the City of Tyre«, immediately recognizes the precise work of a young scholar: While the work is not accompanied with an extensive apparatus of footnotes, he did (as was usual at that time) provide additional notation in parentheses in the body text of the book in order to make his argumentation completely transparent. With studious reference to the sources and textual evidence, he made his arguments comprehensible and verifiable for everyone: The solid researcher does not sit in front of, or on his sources, he opens them up and makes them accessible.[4]

One can learn how to do this very well from Leopold Lucas who was working in this way over a century ago. One can also see the great diligence that went into the work. This is seen, for example, where Lucas was not content merely to lay out the subject matter under investigation. He rather went on to aid his reader by giving his presentation an enormously helpful synoptic overview of the leading figures of the city of Tyre in the twelfth and thirteenth centuries, and this in both the secular and the religious realms.[5] Leopold Lucas also did not shy away from the painstaking work of compiling a table. This is in-

umständliche Begründung einsichtig, und von diesem wissenschaftlichen Werk Leopold Lucas' ist in den verschiedensten Hinsichten auch schon bei den Preisverleihungen vergangener Jahre die Rede gewesen. Lucas' Veröffentlichungen zeichnen sich durch eine ausgesprochen historisch präzise Arbeit aus – wer etwa die Dissertation über »Die Geschichte der Stadt Tyrus« zur Hand nimmt, stellt sofort fest, dass hier ein junger Wissenschaftler am Werk ist, der seine Darstellung zwar (wie damals üblich) noch nicht mit einem umfangreichen Apparat von Fußnoten belegt, der es aber doch durch entsprechende Zusätze und Klammervermerke im Fließtext versteht, seine Argumentation ganz durchsichtig und durch dezidierten Hinweis auf die Quellen und Belege einem jeden nachvollziehbar und nachprüfbar zu machen: Der solide Forscher sitzt nicht vor oder auf seinen Quellen, er öffnet sie, er macht sie zugänglich.[4]

Wie das geht, das kann man bei Leopold Lucas schon vor jetzt mehr als einem Jahrhundert sehr gut lernen. Und man kann auch den großen Fleiß erkennen, der hinter der Arbeit steht, wenn sich Lucas eben nicht damit begnügt hat, den untersuchten Sachverhalt als solchen darzulegen, sondern wenn er seiner Darstellung eine für den interessierten Leser ungemein hilfreiche Ergänzung beigibt durch eine synoptische Übersicht über das im 12. und 13. Jahrhundert in Tyrus im weltlichen wie geistlichen Bereich tätigen Führungspersonal.[5] Die Kärrnerarbeit der Zusammenstellung auch einer solchen sehr praktischen,

deed very practical but it also required a vast amount of detail work!

Leopold Lucas's theological work was done with no less precision. As was already mentioned, he held the office of a rabbi in Glogau. In this service, he concisely brought the aspects of history into relationship with contemporary issues. Already in his inaugural sermon in Glogau, he offered an impressive sample of this based upon Psalm 121:1: »I lift up my eyes to the hills, from where my help comes.«[6]

In this sermon, Lucas first expresses his appreciation for the work of Dr. Benjamin Rippner, his predecessor in the office of the rabbi in Glogau.[7] He does this in such a way that the listener immediately senses recognition and sympathy – not only for the person but also for the way in which he worked: »in his teaching, he [Rippner] proceeded from that which was obvious and, in a logical development, led his audience to always more difficult problems and to always higher viewpoints of the same [–] and this in a way that one could gather an insight into the workshop of his mind where ideas were developed and processed.«[8] Rippner was thus able to compose a single coherent image of Judaism: »And the image presented the individual ideas of Judaism and their development in history as this can only be correctly recognized through an unbiased examination of all of the sources of religious knowledge.«[9] Leopold Lu-

aber eine Unmenge von Detailarbeit erfordernden Tabelle hat Leopold Lucas jedenfalls nicht gescheut!

Und mit nicht weniger Genauigkeit hat Leopold Lucas auch theologisch gearbeitet. Er hat ja, wie schon erwähnt, das Amt eines Rabbiners in Glogau bekleidet. Dabei hat er prägnant die Aspekte der Geschichte mit denen der Gegenwart zueinander in Beziehung gesetzt. Gleich in seiner Antrittspredigt in Glogau hat er davon eine eindrückliche Probe geliefert. Grundgelegt war ihr Psalm 121,1: »Meine Augen erhebe ich zu den Bergen, von dannen mir Hilfe kommt.«[6]

Lucas hat in dieser Predigt zunächst das Wirken Dr. Benjamin Rippners,[7] seines Vorgängers im dortigen Amt des Rabbiners, auf eine Weise gewürdigt, der man sofort Anerkennung und Sympathie abspürt – nicht nur für die Person, sondern auch für die Art und Weise, in der diese am Ort gewirkt hat: »Vom Naheliegenden ging er [Rippner] in seiner Lehre aus[,] und in logischer Entwickelung führte er seine Zuhörer zu immer schwierigeren Problemen und immer höherer Anschauung derselben [–] und das in einer Weise, daß man Einblick nehmen konnte in die Werkstätte seines Geistes, wo Ideen sich entwickelten und verarbeitet wurden.«[8] So habe Rippner ein einheitliches, in sich stimmiges Bild vom Judentum zu entwerfen vermocht: »Und das Bild stellte die einzelnen Ideen des Judentums dar und ihre Entwickelung in der Geschichte, wie diese richtig nur erkannt werden kann durch unbefangene Prüfung aller Quellen

cas did *not* claim that he wanted to emulate his predecessor; yet this is unmistakably inscribed in what he presents in his sermon regarding the interrelationship of faith in God, the moral law and history. Thus Lucas did not shy away from a very sober analysis of the contemporary situation in 1899: »But the flame of faith in God has become weaker and weaker and it usually lightens only as a dull and dying shine.«[10] In analysis of the causes of this, he decisively rejected the »lower motives« of his contemporaries who designed their lives self-confidently and by trusting in their own strength − »modern culture« was much more responsible for the observable destruction of faith in God.[11]

Now, Leopold Lucas would not have been Leopold Lucas if he would have simply asserted this thesis without, at the same time, carefully establishing it − and providing a perspective of the matter that goes beyond it. With the large number of inventions and discoveries came also a change in the traditional understanding of God. This led to an ever rougher criticism which also shook faith in God. Science and philosophy were »subordinate to religion earlier.« »In the modern era they freed themselves entirely from this subordination. As they no longer needed to receive their confirmation from religion, they turned the page and wanted to confirm or reject religion.«[12] Lucas does not remain caught up in this depressing

der religiösen Erkenntnis.«[9] Leopold Lucas hat *nicht* formuliert, dass er es seinem Vorgänger gleichtun wolle – aber dem, was er dann in seiner Predigt entfaltet mit Blick auf den Zusammenhang von Gottesglauben, Sittengesetz und Geschichte ist eben dies doch unverkennbar einbeschrieben. So hat Lucas es nicht gescheut, sehr nüchtern die Gegenwart des Jahres 1899 zu skizzieren: »Aber die Flamme des Gottesglaubens ist immer schwächer und schwächer geworden und leuchtet meistens nur noch als matter ersterbender Glanz.«[10] Bei der Analyse der Ursachen dafür verneint er aber entschieden »niedere Motive« seiner Zeitgenossen, die selbstbewusst und auf ihre Kraft vertrauend ihr Leben gestalteten – verantwortlich für die zu beobachtende Zerstörung des Gottesglaubens sei vielmehr »die moderne Kultur«.[11]

Nun wäre aber Leopold Lucas nicht Leopold Lucas, wenn er diese These nur in den Raum stellte, sie aber nicht sorgsam fundierte – und nicht auch eine Perspektive über sie hinaus zu eröffnen vermöchte. Mit der Vielzahl an Erfindungen und Entdeckungen sei, so Lucas, ein Wandel auch hinsichtlich der hergebrachten Vorstellungen über Gott eingetreten, der zu einer immer schrofferen Kritik geführt habe, die auch den Glauben an Gott erschüttert habe. Naturwissenschaft und Philosophie seien »früher der Religion untergeordnet« gewesen. »Von dieser Unterordnung hatten sie sich in der Neuzeit gründlichst befreit. Als sie aber ihre Bestätigung nicht mehr von der Religion zu erhalten brauchten, da wendeten sie

perspectives, even when he holds: »while the old relationship was a misfortune for science, the new one
became a misfortune for religion.«[13] He rather takes
a decidedly theological perspective that leads out of
this impasse: »What do I think? God does not need
to be proved by science and philosophy because nature and spirit are only images of his power, offspring of the almighty will. Human beings do not
need to prove God through nature and spirit; God
revealed himself through nature and spirit. Accord-
ingly, I want to teach a theology that does not beg
science and philosophy for recognition« – indeed, he
then speaks boldly of a »theology, which is filled with
the consciousness of its own grandeur which is established in the covenant that God made with the priest-
hood in Israel.«[14]

For Leopold Lucas, history, as it is given and lived,
acquires a substantial and characteristic significance
against this background, and this is also – and especially – the case for the present. He therefore sees it
as his task to »proclaim the teaching of all times« and
to »point out to each person again and again and ex-
hort each one again and again to put their soul into
the given content and to include themselves in their

das Blatt um und wollten nun ihrerseits die Religion
bestätigen oder verwerfen.«[12] Lucas bleibt aber nicht
in dieser deprimierenden Perspektive befangen, auch
wenn er konstatiert: »War aber das alte Verhältnis ein
Unglück für die Wissenschaft, so wurde das neue ein
Unglück für die Religion«.[13] Er markiert vielmehr
eine dezidiert theologische Perspektive, die aus dieser
Sackgasse herausführt: »Was ich meine? Gott braucht
nicht von der Naturwissenschaft und Philosophie be-
wiesen zu werden, denn Natur und Geist sind nur
Abbilder seiner Macht, Geburten des allmächtigen
Willens. Die Menschen brauchen Gott nicht zu be-
weisen durch die Natur und den Geist; durch Natur und Geist hat Gott sich offenbart. Und dement-
sprechend will ich eine Theologie lehren, die nicht
um Anerkennung bei Naturwissenschaft und Philosophie bettelt« – ja, er spricht dann steil von einer
»Theologie, die erfüllt ist von dem Bewußtsein ihrer Selbstherrlichkeit, die begründet ist im Bunde,
den Gott geschlossen hat mit dem Priestertum in Israel.«[14]

Und vor diesem Hintergrund gewinnt für Leopold Lucas eben die gegebene, durchlebte Geschichte
eine tragende, prägende Bedeutung auch und gerade
für die Gegenwart, so dass er es als seine Aufgabe an-
sieht, dass er »die Lehre aller Zeiten verkünde« und
dass er »immer wieder und wieder darauf hinweise
und wieder und wieder ermahne, daß ein jeder seine
Seele hineinlege in den gegebenen Inhalt, und daß

own particular way in the chain of the generations of Israel.«[15]

In this way, Leopold Lucas understood his professional work as a rabbi and his academic work as a historian, theologian and philosopher to be closely connected to one another. When two award winners, Angelika Neuwirth and Christian Heinemeyer, will be honored today in the memory of Leopold Lucas's person and work, it can surely be said that both of their accomplishments are not to be described as limited analyses of a few matters, but rather as perspectives that take account of and examine the respective (historical) reality in a comprehensive way.

That Dr. Christian Heinemeyer achieved this in an equally comprehensive and excellent way in his dissertation »Between Empire and Region in the late Middle Ages: Governance and Political Networks around Emperor Frederick III and Elector Albrecht Achilles of Brandenburg«[16] is not only confirmed by the official reviews of the dissertation from the procedures of the doctoral promotion; it is also confirmed best and most impressively by one's own reading of the study. According to the regulations for the granting of the Dr. Leopold Lucas Junior Scholar Prize, the prize is to be awarded for *one* outstanding dissertation, yearly alternating between the fields of Protestant Theology, Catholic Theology, Philosophy and History. In this cycle, in 2015 it was the

ein jeder so auf die ihm eigentümliche Weise sich ein-
reihe in die Kette der Geschlechter Israels.«[15]

Leopold Lucas hat so seine berufliche Aufgabe
als Rabbiner und seine wissenschaftliche Tätigkeit
als Historiker, als Theologe und als Philosoph auf
das Engste aufeinander bezogen verstanden – und
wenn nun heute im Gedächtnis an sein Wirken zwei
Preisträger geehrt werden, Angelika Neuwirth und
Christian Heinemeyer, so kann auf jeden Fall dies
von beider Wirken gesagt werden, dass dieses ebenso
ein Charakteristikum darin trägt, dass es eben nicht
gekennzeichnet ist von einer Engführung auf wenige
zu reflektierende Aspekte, sondern von einer breit
die jeweilige (geschichtliche) Wirklichkeit wahrneh-
menden und durchmusternden Perspektive.

Dass das Herr Dr. Christian Heinemeyer in seiner Dissertation »Zwischen Reich und Region im
Spätmittelalter. Governance und politische Netzwerke um Kaiser Friedrich III. und Kurfürst Albrecht Achilles von Brandenburg«[16] in einer ebenso
umfassenden wie vorzüglichen Weise gelungen ist,
das bestätigen nicht nur die im Zuge des Promotions-
verfahrens erstellten Gutachten, das erweist am aller-
besten und eindrücklichsten die eigene Lektüre seiner Untersuchung. Nach den Bestimmungen über
den Dr. Leopold Lucas-Nachwuchswissenschaftler-
preis wird dieser ja jährlich wechselnd für *eine* hervorragende Dissertation aus den Bereichen entweder der Evangelischen Theologie, der Katholischen
Theologie, der Philosophie oder der Geschichtswis-

turn of the historical studies to submit the proposal for the granting of the prize – and their choice is Dr. Christian Heinemeyer on the basis of his dissertation.

Christian Heinemeyer was also born in Marburg (Lahn). He studied modern history, law and French in Marburg, Aix-en-Provence and here in Tübingen. Following the master's exams in 2011, he began his work on his dissertation (building upon his master's thesis) under the supervision of Prof. Dr. Ellen Widder. As I have been explicitly informed and thus wish to mention here, his second adviser was Prof. Dr. Patzold. Dr. Heinemeyer was, at this time, working as an Academic Collaborator in the Special Research Area 923 »Threatened Orders« in the subproject »Endangerment of Political-Social Orders in the Fourteenth and Fifteenth Century: Dynastic Ruptures«.[17] In 2013, Christian Heinemeyer's dissertation was accepted by the Faculty of Philosophy with the grade *summa cum laude*.

In his work he examines the political networks in the Holy Roman Empire of the German Nation with a special focus on the timeframe from 1470 to 1475. He succeeded in sketching out the existing in-

senschaft vergeben. In diesem Turnus war nun in
diesem Jahr 2015 die Geschichtswissenschaft an der
Reihe, den Vorschlag für die Vergabe des Preises zu
machen – und ihre Wahl ist auf Dr. Christian Heinemeyer um der von ihm vorgelegten Untersuchung
willen gefallen.

Auch er, Christian Heinemeyer, stammt gebürtig
aus Marburg (Lahn). Dortselbst, in Aix-en-Provence
und hier in Tübingen hat er Neuere und Neueste Geschichte, Rechtswissenschaft und Französisch stu-
diert. An das Magisterexamen im Jahr 2011 anschlie-
ßend hat er, betreut von Frau Kollegin Prof. Dr. Ellen Widder, auf seine Magisterarbeit aufbauend, die
Arbeit an seiner Dissertation im Fach Geschichtswissenschaft aufgenommen; er war dabei – darauf bin
ich ausdrücklich hingewiesen worden und will es
darum hier gern auch besonders erwähnen, zweit-
betreut von Herrn Kollegen Prof. Dr. Patzold und
war in dieser Zeit als Wissenschaftlicher Mitarbei-
ter tätig am Sonderforschungsbereich 923 »Bedrohte
Ordnungen« im Teilprojekt »Die Bedrohung poli-
tisch-sozialer Ordnungen im 14./15. Jahrhundert.
Dynastische Brüche«.[17] 2013 ist Christian Heine-
meyers Dissertation dann von der Philosophischen
Fakultät mit dem Prädikat »summa cum laude« angenommen worden.

In seiner Arbeit hat er die politischen Netzwerke
im Heiligen Römischen Reich Deutscher Nation mit
besonderem Fokus auf die Jahre zwischen 1470 und
1475 untersucht. Dabei ist es ihm gelungen, die zu

terconnections and networks for the safeguarding and exercising of governance at territorial and local levels. With this, he analyzed the various interactions between these networks. A complex picture emerges which is fruitful for all aspects of late medieval political history. This could only be achieved on the basis of a very broad study of sources. In order to achieve reliable results, the research also had to be carried out in accordance with a clear analytical classification of these sources. The outcome of this focused and consistent work is a new understanding of the governance of Emperor Frederick III as – in contrast to the *opinio communis* – pragmatic and efficient. With this, a new understanding of this late medieval era has become possible: The imperial-political, foreign-political, regional, local and Imperial City network of interests can now be opened up and the observable governance can be understood as, under the prevailing circumstances, purposeful. Or, to put the matter boldly, with such a precise analysis, Emperor Frederick III does not prove to be »the Holy Roman Empire's arch-sleepyhead,« as he has often been presented in previous historical studies.[18]

Christian Heinemeyer has provided a distinctive impulse through his excellent academic work and shall therefore be awarded the Dr. Leopold Lucas

dieser Zeit bestehenden Geflechte und Netzwerke zur Wahrnehmung und Ausübung der Regierung in ihren territorialen wie lokalen Bezügen und Wechselwirkungen nachzuzeichnen und ein vielschichtiges Bild entstehen zu lassen, das für alle Bereiche der spätmittelalterlichen Politikgeschichte fruchtbar wird. Das konnte nur gelingen auf der Basis eines sehr breit angelegten Quellenstudiums, und es musste, um zu belastbaren Ergebnissen zu kommen, unternommen werden unter Beachtung einer klaren Systematik zu deren Durchmusterung. Der Ertrag dieser konzentriert und konsequent durchgeführten Arbeit ist kein geringerer als der, dass nun das Regierungshandeln Kaiser Friedrichs III. anders als bisher doch als pragmatisch und effizient begriffen werden kann – und damit ein neues Verstehen dieser spätmittelalterlichen Epoche möglich geworden ist: Die reichspolitischen, außenpolitischen, regionalen, lokalen und reichsstädtischen Interessengeflechte können nun erschlossen und das zu beobachtende Regierungshandeln als unter den obwaltenden Verhältnissen zielstrebig begriffen werden. Oder um es plakativ zu sagen: Bei eben einer solchen genauen Betrachtung erweist sich etwa Kaiser Friedrich III. doch nicht als »des heiligen Römischen Reiches Erzschlafmütze«,[18] als die er in der bisherigen Geschichtsschreibung oft dargestellt worden ist.

So hat Christian Heinemeyer durch seine hervorragende wissenschaftliche Arbeit einen markanten Impuls gegeben, und ihm wird deshalb in diesem Jahr

Junior Scholar Prize (which has been awarded since 1985)! Dr. Heinemeyer, I would now like to ask you to receive this prize!

[Reading of the certificate and granting of the prize]

Ladies and Gentlemen,

This year Professor Dr. Dr. h.c. Angelika Neuwirth will be awarded the Dr. Leopold Lucas Prize. She holds the Chair of Arabic Studies in the Department for Semitic and Arabic Studies at the Free University of Berlin. While Berlin continues to be her center of activity, she is not originally from this city: she was born in Nienburg an der Weser. She went on to study classical philology, Oriental, Arabic and Semitic Studies in Göttingen and at the Free University of Berlin and studied outside of Germany as well, in Florence, Tehran and at the Hebrew University in Jerusalem. After completing her Arabic and Islamic studies in Jerusalem with a Master of Arts degree, she devoted herself to doctoral studies at the University of Göttingen where she submitted her dissertation on the Arab reception of Aristotle: »Abdallatif al-Baghdadi's Compendium to Aristotle's *Metaphysics: The Book of Lambda*.« She completed her doctoral studies in 1972.[19]

der seit 1985 vergebene Dr. Leopold Lucas-Nach-
wuchswissenschaftlerpreis verliehen! Sie, Herr Dr.
Heinemeyer, darf ich nun bitten, diese Auszeichnung
in Empfang zu nehmen!

[Verlesung der Urkunde und deren Aushändigung]

Meine sehr verehrten Damen und Herren,

Frau Professorin Dr. Dr. h.c. Angelika Neuwirth
wird in diesem Jahr mit dem Dr. Leopold-Lucas-Preis
ausgezeichnet. Als Inhaberin des Lehrstuhls für Arabistik am Seminar für Semitistik und Arabistik hat
sie an der Freien Universität Berlin gewirkt, und Berlin ist nach wie vor ein Zentrum ihres Wirkens. Ihre
Wiege hat indes nicht dort gestanden, sie ist in Nienburg an der Weser geboren. Das Studium der Klassischen Philologie sowie der Orientwissenschaften,
der Arabistik und Semitistik, führte sie nach Göttingen und an die Freie Universität Berlin, aber auch
bereits weit über Deutschland hinaus nach Florenz,
nach Teheran und an die Hebrew University in Jerusalem. Nachdem sie dort das Studium der Arabistik und Islamwissenschaft mit dem Magister Artium
abschloss, widmete sie sich einer Promotion an der
Georg-August-Universität Göttingen, der sie eine
Dissertation zur arabischen Aristoteles-Rezeption
vorlegte: »Abdallatif al-Baghdadis Kompendium zu
Aristoteles' Metaphysik, Buch Lambda«. 1972 wurde
die Promotion vollzogen.[19]

With »Studies on the Composition of the Meccan Suras« she completed her habilitation in 1977 in Munich in the field of Arabic and Islamic Studies.[20] In the same year, she became a visiting professor of Islamic philosophy in Amman. She taught in Arabic for multiple years; this provided her with an opportunity to engage in the intellectual discourse there and also to have an intensive encounter with contemporary Arab literature.

From 1981 to 1983 she was also a section leader for Quran studies in Jordan at the Aal al-Bayt Foundation for Islamic Civilization until she returned to Germany in 1984. Initially, she held a Heisenberg Professorship in Munich and then, from 1988 onwards, served as Fiebinger-Professor in Bamberg. In 1991, she then became Chair of Arabic Studies at the Free University of Berlin. In an equally challenging and tense situation, she worked as Director of the Orient-Institute of the German Oriental Society from 1994 to 1999 with locations in Istanbul and Beirut. At this time, in Lebanon, the civil war had just ended. In this context at this time, Angelika Neuwirth not only set herself the task of leading the research organization – she also worked in the area of culture and politics.

Mit »Studien zur Komposition der mekkanischen Suren« konnte sie sich 1977 in München für Arabistik und Islamwissenschaft habilitieren[20] und noch im gleichen Jahr eine Gastprofessur für Islamische Philosophie in Amman übernehmen. Mehrere Jahre hatte sie so Gelegenheit, in arabischer Sprache zu lehren — das eröffnete ihr zugleich den Zugang zum dortigen intellektuellen Diskurs und ermöglichte ihr eine intensive Begegnung mit der arabischen Literatur der Gegenwart.

Von 1981 bis 1983 hat sie dann ebenfalls in Jordanien an der Aal al-Bayt-Foundation for Islamic Civilization eine Sektion für Koranstudien geleitet, bis sie 1984 nach Deutschland zurückkehrte, zunächst eine Heisenberg-Professur in München wahrnahm, von 1988 an als Fiebinger-Professorin in Bamberg wirkte, bevor sie dann 1991 an der Freien Universität in Berlin auf den Lehrstuhl für Arabistik berufen wurde. In eine ebenso herausfordernde wie spannungsreiche Situation führte sie die Aufgabe der Direktorin des Orient-Instituts der Deutschen Morgenländischen Gesellschaft in den Jahren von 1994 bis 1999 mit Niederlassungen in Istanbul und in Beirut. Dort, im Libanon, war seinerzeit gerade erst der Bürgerkrieg zu Ende gegangen, und Angelika Neuwirth sah sich damit nicht nur vor die Aufgabe der Forschungsorganisation gestellt, sondern auch, kulturpolitisch aktiv zu werden.

Among Angelika Neuwirth's outstanding achievements, one which is absolutely to be mentioned here, is the large research project *Corpus Coranicum – Text Documentation and Historical-Critical Commentary on the Quran*. This was initiated from 2007 onwards in the context of the Berlin-Brandenburg Academy of Sciences, together with her collaborators Michael Marx and Nicolai Sinai. The project has gained attention far beyond its original goal of being a fundamental academic edition of the central texts of Islam. The project has thus initiated a discourse with Muslim scholars. With this, Angelika Neuwirth has also become a highly regarded consultant for the formation of degree programs in Islamic theology as these have been established in recent years at various universities. She has also been involved in establishing a semester abroad in Jerusalem for Muslim theologians and has contributed to the facilitation of discussions in Islamic theology in Tehran. That Angelika Neuwirth's academic engagement also shows itself in her contributions to the fellow-projects of the Institute for Advanced Study in Berlin, and that she has regularly offered courses at the Dormition Abbey in Jerusalem, and that she has served as the Co-Director of the Center for Literary and Cultural Research, all of this can only be briefly mentioned here.

Zu den herausragenden, unbedingt zu nennenden Erfolgen der Wirksamkeit Angelika Neuwirths gehört es, das Forschungsprojekt »Corpus Coranicum – Textdokumentation und historisch-kritischer Kommentar zum Koran« im Kontext der Berlin-Brandenburgischen Akademie der Wissenschaften von 2007 aufzubauen, gemeinsam mit ihren Mitarbeitern Michael Marx und Nicolai Sinai. Dieses Projekt hat inzwischen Ausstrahlung gewonnen weit über sein eigentliches Anliegen hinaus, eine grundlegende wissenschaftliche Editionsarbeit an dem zentralen Text des Islam zu leisten. Es hat einen Diskurs mit muslimischen Wissenschaftlern aus sich herausgesetzt – und Angelika Neuwirth zu einer geschätzten Beraterin bei der Ausgestaltung islamisch-theologischer Studiengänge, wie sie in den zurückliegenden Jahren an verschiedenen Universitäten etabliert worden sind, werden lassen. So hat sie etwa mitgewirkt bei der Einrichtung eines Auslandssemesters in Jerusalem für islamische Theologen und beigetragen zur Ermöglichung von Diskussionen über Fragen der islamischen Theologie in Teheran. Und dass zum wissenschaftlichen Engagement Angelika Neuwirths auch die Mitwirkung an Fellow-Projekten des Berliner Wissenschaftskollegs gehört, dass sie an der Abtei Dormitio in Jerusalem regelmäßige Lehrkurse gegeben hat, dass sie die Aufgabe einer Co-Direktorin des Zentrums für Literatur- und Kulturforschung wahrgenommen hat – das sei hier zumindest durch eine einfache Erwähnung notiert.

Angelika Neuwirth's diverse engagement has not
gone without recognition, and the awarding of the
Dr. Leopold Lucas Prize is not – and this could hardly
be more of an understatement – the first one that she
has received. In 1996 she was awarded the Federal
Cross of Merit First Class for her contribution to the
cultural cooperation between the Federal Republic
of Germany and the Lebanese Republic. She has received honorary doctorates from the universities of
Bamberg, Salzburg and Basel, and, in the United
States, from Yale University. In addition to this, she
was awarded a Mellon Fellowship at the University
of Chicago. She is also a member of the American
Academy of Arts and Letters, the German National
Academy Leopoldina and the Tunisian Academy of
Arts and Letters. She was also awarded, not least, the
Sigmund-Freud-Prize of the German Academy for
Language and Literature and the Ahmad-Tschele-
by-Prize. All of this shows how broad in scope An-
gelika Neuwirth's work is, and how it has been un-
derstood and received as fruitful and beneficial.

From the various fields of study to which she has
contributed, two areas of her work shall be empha-
sized here that stand out in a special way.

Firstly, there is the area that may be described
as »foundational research on the Quran.« She has
worked in this field from her early years of research
to today. In 2007, in the second expanded edition of

Angelika Neuwirths vielfältiger Einsatz ist nicht ohne Resonanz geblieben, und die Auszeichnung mit dem Dr. Leopold Lucas-Preis ist – mit mehr Understatement kann man es kaum ausdrücken – nicht die erste, die sie erfährt. 1996 wurde ihr das Bundesverdienstkreuz 1. Klasse für ihre Verdienste um die kulturelle Zusammenarbeit zwischen der Bundesrepublik Deutschland und der Libanesischen Republik verliehen. Mit Ehrendoktorwürden ist sie von den Universitäten Bamberg, Salzburg und Basel ausgezeichnet worden, ebenso hat sie in den USA die Universität Yale mit einer solchen bedacht. Hinzu treten ein Mellon-Fellowship an der Universität Chicago, die Mitgliedschaft an der American Academy of Arts and Lettres, die Mitgliedschaft in der Deutschen Nationalakademie Leopoldina sowie an der Académie Tunésienne des Arts et des Lettres – und nicht zuletzt die Auszeichnung mit dem Siegmund-Freud-Preis der Deutschen Akademie für Sprache und Dichtung sowie die Verleihung des Ahmad-Tscheleby-Preises. All dies zeigt, wie breit angelegt und als wie fruchtbar und förderlich das Wirken von Angelika Neuwirth verstanden und aufgenommen wird.

Aus der Vielfalt dessen, was sie vorangebracht hat, sei hier der Fokus auf zwei Arbeitsfelder gerichtet, die in besonderer Weise hervortreten.

Da ist zum einen der Bereich, den man als »Grundlagenforschung zum Koran« bezeichnen könnte. Die Arbeit daran zieht sich durch das Lebenswerk der Preisträgerin kontinuierlich von jungen Jahren bis

her *Studies on the Composition of the Meccan Suras*, Angelika Neuwirth correctly holds that there is »still a lack of fundamental studies on its [the Quran's] emergence and literary form«.[21] Angelika Neuwirth has determinedly advocated for a conscientious philological analysis of the Quran – for only in this way can its theological emphases be identified and worked out in the debates of late antiquity. If the Quran is understood as a »textual condensation of a communication process«[22] then its achievement of a theological contouring in contradistinction to the Christian and especially Jewish argumentation at this time can be seen. Angelika Neuwirth shows which fruits of knowledge can be harvested when one precisely extracts the Medinan additions to the Meccan suras. It thereby becomes possible to understand them as a »critical engagement with the theological positions of learned representatives of the great religions«, indeed, as a reflection a religious conversation.[23] Thus the Quran also had a demonstrable part in the formation of the »great« religions in late antiquity – and is therefore not to be isolated from the Judeo-Christian tradition.[24] The conclusions which may be drawn from such an approach were presented by Angelika Neuwirth in a publication titled *The Quran as a Text of Late Antiquity: A European Approach*.[25] She makes it very clear that an essential element of this cataloguing work was the exchange with colleagues, collaborators and students, and in particular the highly networked cooperation in the project »Europe in

zur Gegenwart hindurch. Mit allem Recht hat Angelika Neuwirth noch 2007, als ihre »Studien zur Komposition der mekkanischen Suren« in 2., erweiterter Auflage erschienen, darauf hingewiesen, dass »noch immer grundlegende Studien zu seiner [des Korans] Genese und literarischen Form« fehlten.[21] Entschieden hat sich Angelika Neuwirth für eine gewissenhafte philologische Untersuchung des Koran eingesetzt – denn nur auf diese Weise können dessen theologische Akzentsetzungen in den Debatten der Spätantike erkannt und herausgearbeitet werden. Wenn aber der Koran so als »textueller Niederschlag eines Kommunikationsprozesses« verstanden wird,[22] dann erschließt sich dessen Leistung einer theologischen Konturierung im Gegenüber zur seinerzeitigen christlichen und insbesondere auch jüdischen Argumentation. Angelika Neuwirth zeigt auf, welche Früchte der Erkenntnis es trägt, wenn man die medinischen Zusätze zu den mekkanischen Suren präzise abhebt – damit wird es möglich, sie als »die Auseinandersetzung mit den theologischen Positionen gelehrter Vertreter der großen Religionen« zu verstehen, ja als Widerspiegelung eines Religionsgesprächs.[23] So hat auch der Koran einen erweislichen Anteil an der Formation der »großen« Religionen in der Spätantike – und ist damit von der christlich-jüdischen Tradition nicht zu isolieren.[24] Die Ergebnisse, die ein solcher Ansatz ermöglicht, hat Angelika Neuwirth dann auch in einer Veröffentlichung unter dem Titel »Der Koran als Text der Spätantike.

the Middle East – the Middle East in Europe«, at the
»Center for Literary and Cultural Research«, with
the researchers and colleagues in the Middle East
who are involved in the *Corpus Coranicum* project and
at the School of Advanced Study in Princeton.[26] The
reconstructed genesis of the Quran texts as proclamation is set out as a key to a proper understanding
of the texts. At its time, the proclamation was understood as »a new and rhetorically plausible answer
to key questions« which »convinced the hearers and
united them into a community which would, soon
thereafter, change the cultural map of the wider region.«[27] In this, Angelika Neuwirth conscientiously
integrates the hermeneutical tradition of Islamic
scholarship, which requires intensive collaboration
with Muslim scholars.[28] The texts are to be located
in their specific cultural milieu and a chronological
order is to be established.[29] Upon this framework,
the pre-redactional, post-redactional and canonical
texts can be separated from one another and a historical line of development of the proclamation can be
traced.[30] This historical-literary approach necessarily requires interdisciplinary work[31] – and this is, as
mentioned above, the practice of the academy project
Corpus Coranicum.

Ein europäischer Zugang«[25] aufzuzeigen vermocht.
Sehr deutlich stellt sie heraus, dass ein wesentliches
Moment einer solchen Erschließungsarbeit der Austausch mit Kollegen, Mitarbeitern und Studierenden
war – und dabei insbesondere die intensiv vernetzte
Zusammenarbeit im Rahmen des Projektes »Europe
in the Middle East – the Middle East in Europe«, im
»Zentrum für Literatur- und Kulturforschung«, mit
den am Projekt »Corpus Coranicum« beteiligten
Forschern und Kolleginnen und Kollegen im Nahen
Osten und an der School of Advanced Study in Princeton.[26] Als Schlüssel zu einem angemessenen Verstehen der Korantexte wird deren rekonstruierte Genese als Verkündigung freigelegt – die zu ihrer Zeit
als »eine neue und rhetorisch plausible Antwort auf
zentrale Fragen« verstanden wurden und die »seine
Hörer überzeugte und sie zu einer Gemeinde ver-
einigte, die schon kurze Zeit später die kulturelle
Landkarte der weiteren Region verändern sollte.«[27]
Dabei bezieht Angelika Neuwirth auch bewusst die
hermeneutische Tradition islamischer Gelehrsamkeit
mit ein – was eben eine intensive Zusammenarbeit
mit muslimischen Gelehrten erfordert.[28] Die Texte
sind in ihrem je spezifischen kulturellen Milieu zu
verorten,[29] und es ist auch eine chronologische Ord-
nung herzustellen, vor deren Hintergrund erst es gelingen kann, vor-redaktionellen, nach-redaktionel-
len und kanonischen Text voneinander abzuheben
und so eine geschichtliche Linie der Entwicklung
der Verkündigung nachzuzeichnen.[30] Dieser histo-

Angelika Neuwirth has not only set out distinctive accents that are advancing the academic discourse, she has also contributed to the analysis of modern Arabic literature[32] – such as the work of the Palestinian Mahmoud Darwish and his reception of Biblical books such as Genesis, Exodus and the Song of Songs.[33] This follows from the realization that in Arabic studies it is not sufficient to address exclusively classical, pre-modern texts in the intellectual encounter with the Arab world. Especially since the last quarter of the twentieth century, the numerous conflicts in the context of the Palestinian-Israeli confrontations, and others in the Middle East, have left impressions on modern Arabic literature. In many cases, however, these have not been recognized in the European discourses. Through her participation at the Center for Literary and Cultural Research, Angelika Neuwirth has enabled the transformation of this situation in the academic context. In this, numerous translations have been made available in German and English which provide access to this literature. Furthermore, this literature is now being investigated with the methods of cultural studies. In this regard, she prepared the way for the study of both Palestinian poetry and the literature of the Israeli-Palestinian conflict.

risch-literaturwissenschaftliche Zugang aber erfordert unbedingt eine disziplinübergreifende Arbeit —[31] wie sie denn in dem schon erwähnten Akademieprojekt »Corpus Coranicum« geleistet wird.

Angelika Neuwirth hat nicht nur in diesem Sektor markante, weiterführende Akzente gesetzt, sie hat sich auch der Analyse moderner arabischer Literatur gewidmet —[32] etwa dem Werk des Palästinensers Mahmud Darwisch und dessen Rezeption biblischer Bücher wie der Genesis, des Exodus und des Hoheliedes.[33] Dahinter stand die Erkenntnis, dass es bei der intellektuellen Begegnung mit der arabischen Welt nicht hinreichen kann, sich in der Arabistik weiterhin allein mit klassischen, vormodernen Texten zu befassen. Besonders seit dem letzten Viertel des 20. Jahrhunderts haben die zahlreichen Konfliktlagen und -situationen im Kontext der palästinisch-israelischen Auseinandersetzungen sowie anderer Konfrontationen im Bereich des Nahen Ostens auch markante Spuren in der modernen arabischen Literatur hinterlassen, die aber in den in Europa geführten Diskursen oft kaum Beachtung gefunden haben. Durch ihre Mitarbeit im Zentrum für Literatur- und Kulturforschung hat Angelika Neuwirth dafür gesorgt, dass sich dies im wissenschaftlichen Kontext geändert hat, so dass inzwischen nicht nur zahlreiche Übersetzungen in deutscher und englischer Sprache vorliegen, die zu solcher Literatur Zugang eröffnen, sondern auch diese Literatur nunmehr mit den Methoden der Kulturwissenschaft untersucht wird. So hat sie der

Angelika Neuwirth has thus contributed to the dialog between Islam, Judaism and Christianity in a double sense: Both with view to the past, and, no less, with view to the present. She therefore meets – in a truly excellent, indeed, in a brilliant way – the concern which is connected to this prize. As Consul General Franz D. Lucas, who initiated the foundation of this prize on the occasion of the 100th birthday of his Father, specified, the prize shall honor those personalities who have distinguished themselves through excellent accomplishments in the fields of theology, history and philosophy in a special way for the understanding between human beings and peoples and for the promotion of the concept of tolerance.[34] According to the entirely unanimous decision of the award committee, Angelika Neuwirth has accomplished precisely this! I would therefore now like to ask you to receive the certificate which was prepared for the awarding of this prize.

Erforschung der palästinischen Dichtung und der Literatur des israelisch-palästinensischen Konflikts einen Weg bereitet.

So trägt Angelika Neuwirth in einer doppelten Weise zum Dialog zwischen Islam, Judentum und Christentum bei – mit Blick auf die Vergangenheit, und nicht weniger auch mit Blick auf die Gegenwart. Sie wird damit dem Anliegen, das mit der Vergabe des Dr. Leopold Lucas-Preises verbunden ist, auf eine wirklich hervorragende, ja brillante Weise gerecht – dem Anliegen, Generalkonsul Franz D. Lucas, der die Stiftung dieses Preises aus Anlass des 100. Geburtstags seines Vaters initiiert hat, einst die Kontur gegeben hat, dass durch diesen Preis solche Persönlichkeiten gewürdigt werden, die sich auf den Gebieten der Theologie, der historischen Geisteswissenschaften und Philosophie durch hervorragende Leistungen in besonderer Weise um die Verständigung zwischen Menschen und Völkern sowie um die Verbreitung des Toleranzgedankens verdient gemacht haben.[34] Das hat Angelika Neuwirth nach ganz einmütiger Überzeugung des Vergabeausschusses getan! Und deshalb möchte ich sie nun bitten, die zur Verleihung des Preises gefertigte Urkunde in Empfang nehmen:

[Reading of the certificate followed by granting of the prize]

Congratulations, Prof. Neuwirth! We are looking forward to your lecture!

[Verlesung der Urkunde mit anschließender Über-
reichung]

Eine herzliche Gratulation, sehr verehrte Frau Neuwirth, zu diesem Preis! Und nun sind wir gespannt
auf Ihren Festvortrag!

Notes

1 Leopold Lucas, *Geschichte der Stadt Tyrus zur Zeit der Kreuzzüge* (Berlin: Mayer & Müller, 1896).

2 Leopold Lucas, *Zur Geschichte der Juden im vierten Jahrhundert* (*Beiträge zur Geschichte der Juden* 1; Berlin: Mayer & Müller, 1910).

3 Further to Leopold Lucas's biography, see »Lebenslauf von Rabbiner Dr. Leopold Lucas,« in *Dr. Leopold-Lucas-Stiftung. Statut* (Tübingen 1980), [5]-[7]. Cf. Hanno Drechsler, »Rede in der Feierstunde am 5. März 1986 anläßlich der Umbenennung der Schwangasse in Leopold Lucas-Straße«, in *Rabbiner Dr. Leopold Lucas. Marburg 1872 – 1943 Theresienstadt. Versuch einer Würdigung* (*Marburger Stadtschriften zur Geschichte und Kultur* 21), ed. Erhart Dettmering (Marburg: Presseamt der Stadt Marburg, 1987), 9–14, here: 9–11.

4 Cf. Lucas, *Tyrus* (see note 1), 7–73.

5 Ibid., 81–88.

6 Leopold Lucas, »Meine Augen erhebe ich zu den Bergen, von dannen mir Hilfe kommt«, Psalm 121:1; in *Rabbiner Dr. Leopold Lucas. Marburg 1872 – 1943 Theresienstadt. Versuch einer Würdigung* (*Marburger Stadtschriften zur Geschichte und Kultur* 21), ed. Erhart Dettmering (Marburg: Presseamt der Stadt Marburg, 1987), 27–34, here: 27.

7 Rippner's work and influence in Glogau is briefly addressed by Margret Heitmann, »›Mein Leben begann also damit, daß ich zu Festung verurteilt wurde.‹ Arnold Zweig und seine Geburtsstadt Glogau«, in *Deutscher, Jude, Europäer im 20. Jahrhundert. Arnold Zweig und das Judentum* (*Jahrbuch für internationale Germanistik* A, 65), ed. Julia Bernhard (Bern: Lang, 2004), 34.

8 Lucas, »Meine Augen erhebe ich zu den Bergen« (see note 6), 27.

9 Ibid.

10 Ibid., 30.

11 Ibid.

12 Ibid.

13 Ibid., 30 f.

14 Ibid., 31.

15 Ibid., 34.

16 Published by Duncker & Humblot, Berlin 2016, in »Historische Forschungen« series, volume 108.

Anmerkungen

1 Lucas, Leopold: Geschichte der Stadt Tyrus zur Zeit der Kreuzzüge. Berlin 1896.

2 Lucas, Leopold: Zur Geschichte der Juden im vierten Jahrhundert. Berlin 1910. [= Beiträge zur Geschichte der Juden 1].

3 Zum Lebensweg Leopold Lucas' siehe: Lebenslauf von Rabbiner Dr. Leopold Lucas. In: Dr. Leopold-Lucas-Stiftung. Statut. Tübingen 1980. S. [5]–[7]. Vgl. Drechsler, Hanno: Rede in der Feierstunde am 5. März 1986 anläßlich der Umbenennung der Schwangasse in Leopold Lucas-Straße. In: Dettmering, Erhart (Hgg.): Rabbiner Dr. Leopold Lucas. Marburg 1872 – 1943 Theresienstadt. Versuch einer Würdigung. Marburg 1987. [= Marburger Stadtschriften zur Geschichte und Kultur 21] S. 9–14, dort S. 9–11.

4 S. Lucas, Tyrus (wie Anm. 1), S. 7–73.

5 S. a. a. O., S. 81–88.

6 Lucas, Leopold: »Meine Augen erhebe ich zu den Bergen, von dannen mir Hilfe kommt.« Psalm 121,1. In: Dettmering, Erhart (Hgg.): Rabbiner Dr. Leopold Lucas. Marburg 1872 – 1943 Theresienstadt. Versuch einer Würdigung. Marburg 1987. [= Marburger Stadtschriften zur Geschichte und Kultur 21] S. 27–34, dort S. 27.

7 Rippners Wirken in Glogau ist knapp charakterisiert bei Heitmann, Margret: »Mein Leben begann also damit, daß ich zu Festung verurteilt wurde.« Arnold Zweig und seine Geburtsstadt Glogau. In: Bernhard, Julia (Hg.): Deutscher, Jude, Europäer im 20. Jahrhundert. Arnold Zweig und das Judentum. Bern [u.a.] 2004. [= Jahrbuch für internationale Germanistik A, 65], S. 34.

8 Lucas, Augen (wie Anm. 6), S. 27.

9 Ebd.

10 A. a. O., S. 30.

11 Ebd.

12 Ebd.

13 A. a. O., S. 30 f.

14 A. a. O., S. 31.

15 A. a. O., S. 34.

16 Erschienen bei Duncker & Humblot, Berlin 2016, als Bd. 108 der Reihe »Historische Forschungen«.

17 See Christian Heinemeyer, Iris Holzwart-Schäfer and Ellen Widder, eds., *Geboren, um zu herrschen? Gefährdete Dynastien in historisch–interdisziplinärer Perspektive* (*Bedrohte Ordnungen*) (Tübingen: Mohr Siebeck, 2015).

18 Astrid Schwerhoff, »*Des Heiligen Römischen Reichs Erzschlafmütze«? Historische Urteile über Kaiser Friedrich III. und ihre möglichen Hintergründe* (München 2010). The opinion of Karl Koch, which is summarized in one sentence, may serve as an example of the prevalent characterization of Friedrich III: »While he [Friedrich III] was a good manager of the Habsburg power base, he was indeed no man of imperial dimensions.« Karl Koch, *Kleine Deutsche Kirchengeschichte* (Köln: Bachem, 1940), 108.

19 Published with the title: Angelika Neuwirth, *'Abd al-laṭīf al-Baġdādī's Bearbeitung von Buch Lambda der Aristotelischen Metaphysik* (*Akademie der Wissenschaften und der Literatur XXVII*; Wiesbaden: Steiner, 1976).

20 Angelika Neuwirth, *Studien zur Komposition der mekkanischen Suren* (*Studien zur Sprache, Geschichte und Kultur des islamischen Orients Neue Folge* 10; Berlin: de Gruyter, 1981).

21 Angelika Neuwirth, *Studien zur Komposition der mekkanischen Suren. Die literarische Form des Koran – ein Zeugnis seiner Historizität?* 2., durch eine korangeschichtliche Einführung erweiterte Auflage (*Studien zur Sprache, Geschichte und Kultur des islamischen Orients Neue Folge* 10; Berlin/New York: de Gruyter, 2007), v.

22 Ibid., xxx.

23 Ibid., 53★.

24 Ibid., 53 f.

25 Angelika Neuwirth, *Der Koran als Text der Spätantike: Ein europäischer Zugang*, 3rd ed. (Berlin: Verlag der Weltreligionen, 2013).

26 Ibid., 16 f.

27 Ibid., 20.

28 Ibid., 24.

29 Ibid., 48.

30 Ibid., 48 f.

31 Ibid., 58.

32 Cf. Angelika Neuwirth, ed., *Arabische Literatur, postmodern* (München: Ed. Text + Kritik, 2004); idem, ed., *Arabic literature: Postmodern perspectives* (London: Saqi Books, 2010).

17 S. dazu Heinemeyer, Christian/Holzwart-Schäfer, Iris/Widder, Ellen (Hgg.): Geboren, um zu herrschen? Gefährdete Dynastien in historisch-interdisziplinärer Perspektive. Tübingen 2015. [= Bedrohte Ordnungen].

18 Schwerhoff, Astrid: »Des Heiligen Römischen Reichs Erzschlafmütze«? Historische Urteile über Kaiser Friedrich III. und ihre möglichen Hintergründe. München 2010. Als Beispiel für die gängige Charakterisierung Friedrichs III. mag das auf einen einzigen Satz komprimierte Urteil von Karl Koch dienen: »Wenn er [Friedrich III.] auch ein guter Verwalter der habsburgischen Hausmacht war, so war er doch kein Mann von kaiserlichem Format.« S. Koch, Karl: Kleine Deutsche Kirchengeschichte. Köln 1940. S. 108.

19 Erschienen unter dem Titel: Neuwirth, Angelika: ʿAbd allaṭīf al-Baġdādī's Bearbeitung von Buch Lambda der Aristotelischen Metaphysik. Wiesbaden 1976. [= Akademie der Wissenschaften und der Literatur XXVII].

20 Neuwirth, Angelika: Studien zur Komposition der mekkanischen Suren. Berlin, New York 1981. [= Studien zur Sprache, Geschichte und Kultur des islamischen Orients Neue Folge 10].

21 Neuwirth, Angelika: Studien zur Komposition der mekkanischen Suren. Die literarische Form des Koran – ein Zeugnis seiner Historizität? 2., durch eine korangeschichtliche Einführung erweiterte Auflage. Berlin, New York 2007. [= Studien zur Sprache, Geschichte und Kultur des islamischen Orients Neue Folge 10], S. V.

22 A. a. O., S. XXX.

23 A. a. O., S. 53*.

24 A. a. O., S. 53 f.

25 Neuwirth, Angelika: Der Koran als Text der Spätantike. Ein europäischer Zugang. 3. Aufl. Berlin 2013.

26 A. a. O., S. 16 f.

27 A. a. O., S. 20.

28 A. a. O., S. 24.

29 A. a. O., S. 48.

30 A. a. O., S. 48 f.

31 A. a. O., S. 58.

32 S. dazu etwa Neuwirth, Angelika (Hg.): Arabische Literatur, postmodern. München 2004. – Neuwirth, Angelika (Hg.): Arabic literature. Postmodern perspectives. London 2010.

33 Cf. Angelika Neuwirth, »Kulturelle Sprachbarrieren zwischen Nachbarn. Ein neues Gedicht von Maḥmûd Darwîsh im Verhör seiner israelischen Leser«, in *Orient* 29 (1988), 440–466; idem, »Imagining autobiography: Mahmud Darwish, his poetic persona, and his audience«, in *Autobiographical themes in Turkish literature: Theoretical and comparative perspectives*, eds. Olcay Akyıldız, Halim Kara and Börte Sagaster (*Istanbuler Texte und Studien* 6; Würzburg: Ergon-Verlag, 2007), 203–217; idem, »The Hebrew Bible and Arabic poetry – poetry translating the other's canon: Maḥmûd Darwîsh's project of reading the Hebrew Bible to reclaim Arab memory in Palestine«, in *Poetry and history: The value of poetry in reconstructing Arab history*, ed. Ramzi Baalbaki (Beirut: American University of Beirut Press, 2011), 315–334.

34 Cf. Dr. Leopold-Lucas-Stiftung, *Statut* (Tübingen 1980), § 1, subparagraph 2.

33 S. Neuwirth, Angelika: Kulturelle Sprachbarrieren zwischen Nachbarn. Ein neues Gedicht von Maḥmûd Darwîsh im Verhör seiner israelischen Leser. In: Orient 29 (1988), S. 440–466. – Neuwirth, Angelika: Imagining autobiography: Mahmud Darwish, his poetic persona, and his audience. In: Olcay Akyıldız/Halim Kara/Börte Sagaster (Hgg.): Autobiographical themes in Turkish literature. Theoretical and comparative perspectives. Würzburg 2007. [= Istanbuler Texte und Studien 6], S. 203–217. – Neuwirth, Angelika: The Hebrew Bible and Arabic poetry – poetry translating the other's canon. Ma mūd Darwīsh's project of reading the Hebrew Bible to reclaim Arab memory in Palestine, in: Ramzi Baalbaki (Hg.): Poetry and history. The value of poetry in reconstructing Arab history. Beirut 2011, S. 315–334.

34 Vgl. Dr. Leopold-Lucas-Stiftung. Statut. Tübingen 1980. § 1 Absatz 2.

Die bisherigen Preisträger

2001   Michael Theunissen
2002   Moshe Zimmermann
2003   Martin Gilbert
2004   Sadik J. Al-Azm
2005   Yosef Hayim Yerushalmi
2006   René Girard
2007   Eduard Lohse
2008   Dieter Henrich
2009   Karen Armstrong
2010   Peter L. Berger
2011   Avishai Margalit
2012   Seyla Benhabib
2013   Giorgio Agamben
2014   Peter Schäfer
2015   Angelika Neuwirth